PostgreSQL Development Essentials

Develop programmatic functions to create powerful database applications

Manpreet Kaur
Baji Shaik

BIRMINGHAM - MUMBAI

PostgreSQL Development Essentials

First published: September 2016

Production reference: 1200916

Published by Packt Publishing Ltd.
Livery Place
35 Livery Street
Birmingham
B3 2PB, UK.

ISBN 978-1-78398-900-3

www.packtpub.com

Credits

Authors

Manpreet Kaur

Baji Shaik

Reviewers

Daniel Durante

Danny Sauer

Commissioning Editor

Julian Ursell

Acquisition Editor

Nitin Dasan

Content Development Editor

Anish Sukumaran

Technical Editor

Sunith Shetty

Copy Editor

Zainab Bootwala

Project Coordinator

Izzat Contractor

Proofreader

Safis Editing

Indexer

Rekha Nair

Graphics

Jason Monteiro

Production Coordinator

Aparna Bhagat

About the Authors

Manpreet Kaur currently works as a business intelligence solution developer at an IT-based MNC in Chandigarh. She has over 7 years of work experience in the field of developing successful analytical solutions in data warehousing, analytics and reporting, and portal and dashboard development in the PostgreSQL and Oracle databases. She has worked on business intelligence tools such as Noetix, SSRS, Tableau, and OBIEE. She has a good understanding of ETL tools such as Informatica and Oracle Data Integrator (ODI). Currently, she works on analytical solutions using Hadoop and OBIEE 12c.

Additionally, she is very creative and enjoys oil painting. She also has a youtube channel, *Oh so homemade*, where she posts easy ways to make recycled crafts.

Baji Shaik is a database administrator and developer. He is currently working as a database consultant at OpenSCG. He has an engineering degree in telecommunications, and he started his career as a C# and Java developer. He started working with databases in 2011 and, over the years, he has worked with Oracle, PostgreSQL, and Greenplum. His background spans a wide depth and breadth of expertise and experience in SQL/NoSQL database technologies. He has architectured and designed many successful database solutions addressing challenging business requirements. He has provided solutions using PostgreSQL for reporting, business intelligence, data warehousing, applications, and development support. He has a good knowledge of automation, orchestration, and DevOps in a cloud environment.

He comes from a small village named Vutukutu in Andhra Pradesh and currently lives in Hyderabad. He likes to watch movies, read books, and write technical blogs. He loves to spend time with family. He has tech-reviewed *Troubleshooting PostgreSQL* by Packt Publishing. He is a certified PostgreSQL professional.

Thanks to my loving parents. Thanks to Packt Publishing for giving me this opportunity. Special thanks to Izzat Contractor for choosing me, and Anish Sukumaran, Nitin Dasan, and Sunith Shetty for working with me. Thanks to Dinesh Kumar for helping me write.

About the Reviewers

Daniel Durante started spending time with computers at the age of 12. He has built applications for various sectors, such as the medical industry, universities, the manufacturing industry, and the open source community. He mainly uses Golang, C, Node, or PHP for developing web applications, frameworks, tools, embedded systems, and so on. Some of his personal work can be found on GitHub and his personal website.

He has also worked on the *PostgreSQL Developer's Guide*, published by Packt Publishing.

> *I would like to thank my parents, brother, and friends, who've all put up with my insanity, day in and day out. I would not be here today if it weren't for their patience, guidance, and love.*

Danny Sauer has been a Linux sysadmin, software developer, security engineer, open source advocate, and general computer geek at various companies for around 20 years. He has administered, used, and programmed PostgreSQL for over half of that time. When he's not building solutions in the digital world, he and his wife enjoy restoring their antique home and teaching old cars new tricks.

www.PacktPub.com

eBooks, discount offers, and more

Did you know that Packt offers eBook versions of every book published, with PDF and ePub files available? You can upgrade to the eBook version at www.PacktPub.com and as a print book customer, you are entitled to a discount on the eBook copy. Get in touch with us at customercare@packtpub.com for more details.

At www.PacktPub.com, you can also read a collection of free technical articles, sign up for a range of free newsletters and receive exclusive discounts and offers on Packt books and eBooks.

https://www2.packtpub.com/books/subscription/packtlib

Do you need instant solutions to your IT questions? PacktLib is Packt's online digital book library. Here, you can search, access, and read Packt's entire library of books.

Why subscribe?

- Fully searchable across every book published by Packt
- Copy and paste, print, and bookmark content
- On demand and accessible via a web browser

Table of Contents

Preface   1

Chapter 1: Advanced SQL   5

  Creating views   5
    Deleting and replacing views   7
  Materialized views   8
    Why materialized views?   8
      Read-only, updatable, and writeable materialized views   8
      Read-only materialized views   9
      Updatable materialized views   9
      Writeable materialized views   10
  Creating cursors   10
    Using cursors   11
    Closing a cursor   12
  Using the GROUP BY clause   12
  Using the HAVING clause   14
    Parameters or arguments   14
  Using the UPDATE operation clauses   15
  Using the LIMIT clause   15
  Using subqueries   16
  Subqueries that return multiple rows   18
    Correlated subqueries   18
    Existence subqueries   19
    Parameters or arguments   19
  Using the Union join   20
  Using the Self join   21
  Using the Outer join   22
    Left outer join   23
    Right outer join   24
    Full outer join   24
  Summary   26

Chapter 2: Data Manipulation   27

  Conversion between datatypes   27
  Introduction to arrays   28
    Array constructors   28

String_to_array()	31
Array_dims( )	32
ARRAY_AGG()	32
ARRAY_UPPER()	34
Array_length()	34
Array slicing and splicing	34
UNNESTing arrays to rows	35
Introduction to JSON	37
Inserting JSON data in PostgreSQL	37
Querying JSON	38
Equality operation	38
Containment	38
Key/element existence	39
Outputting JSON	40
Using XML in PostgreSQL	41
Inserting XML data in PostgreSQL	41
Querying XML data	42
Composite datatype	42
Creating composite types in PostgreSQL	42
Altering composite types in PostgreSQL	44
Dropping composite types in PostgreSQL	45
Summary	45
Chapter 3: Triggers	47
Introduction to triggers	47
Adding triggers to PostgreSQL	48
Modifying triggers in PostgreSQL	53
Removing a trigger function	54
Creating a trigger function	55
Testing the trigger function	56
Viewing existing triggers	57
Summary	58
Chapter 4: Understanding Database Design Concepts	59
Basic design rules	59
The ability to solve the problem	59
The ability to hold the required data	60
The ability to support relationships	60
The ability to impose data integrity	60
The ability to impose data efficiency	60
The ability to accommodate future changes	60
Normalization	61
Anomalies in DBMS	61

First normal form	63
Second normal form	63
Third normal form	64
Common patterns	65
Many-to-many relationships	65
Hierarchy	66
Recursive relationships	67
Summary	68

Chapter 5: Transactions and Locking — 69

Defining transactions	69
ACID rules	70
Effect of concurrency on transactions	71
Transactions and savepoints	71
Transaction isolation	72
Implementing isolation levels	73
Dirty reads	73
Non-repeatable reads	74
Phantom reads	75
ANSI isolation levels	75
Transaction isolation levels	76
Changing the isolation level	76
Using explicit and implicit transactions	77
Avoiding deadlocks	77
Explicit locking	78
Locking rows	78
Locking tables	79
Summary	80

Chapter 6: Indexes and Constraints — 83

Introduction to indexes and constraints	83
Primary key indexes	84
Unique indexes	85
B-tree indexes	86
Standard indexes	87
Full text indexes	88
Partial indexes	88
Multicolumn indexes	90
Hash indexes	91
GIN and GiST indexes	91
Clustering on an index	92
Foreign key constraints	93

Unique constraints	94
Check constraints	96
NOT NULL constraints	97
Exclusion constraints	98
Summary	98
Chapter 7: Table Partitioning	99
Table partitioning	99
Partition implementation	104
Partitioning types	109
List partition	109
Managing partitions	111
Adding a new partition	111
Purging an old partition	112
Alternate partitioning methods	113
Method 1	113
Method 2	114
Constraint exclusion	116
Horizontal partitioning	118
PL/Proxy	119
Foreign inheritance	120
Summary	123
Chapter 8: Query Tuning and Optimization	125
Query tuning	125
Hot versus cold cache	126
Cleaning the cache	127
pg_buffercache	130
pg_prewarm	132
Optimizer settings for cached data	133
Multiple ways to implement a query	135
Bad query performance with stale statistics	137
Optimizer hints	139
Explain Plan	144
Generating and reading the Explain Plan	144
Simple example	145
More complex example	145
Query operators	146
Seq Scan	146
Index Scan	146
Sort	147
Unique	147

LIMIT	147
Aggregate	147
Append	147
Result	147
Nested Loop	148
Merge Join	148
Hash and Hash Join	148
Group	148
Subquery Scan and Subplan	148
Tid Scan	148
Materialize	149
Setop	149
Summary	149
Chapter 9: PostgreSQL Extensions and Large Object Support	151
Creating an extension	151
Compiling extensions	153
Database links in PostgreSQL	154
Using binary large objects	157
Creating a large object	158
Importing a large object	158
Exporting a large object	159
Writing data to a large object	159
Server-side functions	159
Summary	160
Chapter 10: Using PHP in PostgreSQL	161
Postgres with PHP	161
PHP-to-PostgreSQL connections	162
Dealing with DDLs	165
DML operations	166
pg_query_params	167
pg_insert	168
Data retrieval	169
pg_fetch_all	169
pg_fetch_assoc	170
pg_fetch_result	171
Helper functions to deal with data fetching	172
pg_free_results	172
pg_num_rows	172

pg_num_fields	172
pg_field_name	172
pg_meta_data	172
pg_convert	173
UPDATE	175
DELETE	176
COPY	176
Summary	178
Chapter 11: Using Java in PostgreSQL	179
Making database connections to PostgreSQL using Java	179
Using Java to create a PostgreSQL table	182
Using Java to insert records into a PostgreSQL table	183
Using Java to update records into a PostgreSQL table	184
Using Java to delete records into a PostgreSQL table	185
Catching exceptions	186
Using prepared statements	188
Loading data using COPY	188
Connection properties	190
Summary	191
Index	193

Preface

The purpose of this book is to teach you the fundamental practices and techniques of database developers for programming database applications with PostgreSQL. It is targeted to database developers using PostgreSQL who have basic experience developing database applications with the system, but want a deeper understanding of how to implement programmatic functions with PostgreSQL.

What this book covers

Chapter 1, *Advanced SQL*, aims to help you understand advanced SQL topics such as views, materialized views, and cursors and will be able to get a sound understanding of complex topics such as subqueries and joins.

Chapter 2, *Data Manipulation*, provides you the ability to perform data type conversions and perform JSON and XML operations in PostgreSQL.

Chapter 3, *Triggers*, explains how to perform trigger operations and use trigger functions in PostgreSQL.

Chapter 4, *Understanding Database Design Concepts*, explains data modeling and normalization concepts. The reader will then be able to efficiently create a robust database design.

Chapter 5, *Transactions and Locking*, covers the effect of transactions and locking on the database. The reader will also be able to understand isolation levels and understand multi-version concurrency control behavior.

Chapter 6, *Indexes And Constraints*, provides knowledge about the different indexes and constraints available in PostgreSQL. This knowledge will help the reader while coding and the reader will be in a better position to choose among the different indexes and constraints depending upon the requirement during the coding phase.

Chapter 7, *Table Partitioning*, gives the reader a better understanding of partitioning in PostgreSQL. The reader will be able to use the different partitioning methods available in PostgreSQL and also implement horizontal partitioning using PL/Proxy.

Chapter 8, *Query Tuning and Optimization*, provides knowledge about different mechanisms and approaches available to tune a query. The reader will be able to utilize this knowledge in order to write a optimal/efficient query or code.

Chapter 9, *PostgreSQL Extensions and Large Object Support*, will familiarize the reader with the concept of extensions in PostgreSQL and also with the usage of large objects' datatypes in PostgreSQL.

Chapter 10, *Using PHP in PostgreSQL*, covers the basics of performing database operations in PostgreSQL using the PHP language, which helps reader to start with PHP code.

Chapter 11, *Using Java in PostgreSQL*, this chapter provides knowledge about database connectivity using Java and creating/modifying objects using Java code. It also talks about JDBC drivers.

What you need for this book

You need PostgreSQL 9.4 or higher to be installed on your machine to test the codes provided in the book. As this covers Java and PHP, you need Java and PHP binaries installed on your machine. All other tools covered in this book have installation procedures included, so there's no need to install them before you start reading the book.

Who this book is for

This book is mainly for PostgreSQL developers who want to develop applications using programming languages. It is also useful for tuning databases through query optimization, indexing, and partitioning.

Conventions

In this book, you will find a number of text styles that distinguish between different kinds of information. Here are some examples of these styles and an explanation of their meaning.

Code words in text, database table names, folder names, filenames, file extensions, pathnames, dummy URLs, user input, and Twitter handles are shown as follows: "Database views are created using the CREATE VIEW statement. "

A block of code is set as follows:

```
import java.sql.Connection;
import java.sql.DriverManager;
import java.sql.Statement;
import java.sql.ResultSet;
import java.sql.SQLException;
```

Any command-line input or output is written as follows:

```
CREATE VIEW view_name AS
SELECT column1, column2
FROM table_name
WHERE [condition];
```

New terms and **important words** are shown in bold.

 Warnings or important notes appear in a box like this.

 Tips and tricks appear like this.

Reader feedback

Feedback from our readers is always welcome. Let us know what you think about this book—what you liked or disliked. Reader feedback is important for us as it helps us develop titles that you will really get the most out of. To send us general feedback, simply e-mail feedback@packtpub.com, and mention the book's title in the subject of your message. If there is a topic that you have expertise in and you are interested in either writing or contributing to a book, see our author guide at www.packtpub.com/authors.

Customer support

Now that you are the proud owner of a Packt book, we have a number of things to help you to get the most from your purchase.

Errata

Although we have taken every care to ensure the accuracy of our content, mistakes do happen. If you find a mistake in one of our books-maybe a mistake in the text or the code-we would be grateful if you could report this to us. By doing so, you can save other readers from frustration and help us improve subsequent versions of this book. If you find any errata, please report them by visiting http://www.packtpub.com/submit-errata, selecting your book, clicking on the **Errata Submission Form** link, and entering the details of your errata. Once your errata are verified, your submission will be accepted and the errata will be uploaded to our website or added to any list of existing errata under the Errata section of that title.

To view the previously submitted errata, go to https://www.packtpub.com/books/content/support and enter the name of the book in the search field. The required information will appear under the **Errata** section.

Piracy

Piracy of copyrighted material on the Internet is an ongoing problem across all media. At Packt, we take the protection of our copyright and licenses very seriously. If you come across any illegal copies of our works in any form on the Internet, please provide us with the location address or website name immediately so that we can pursue a remedy.

Please contact us at copyright@packtpub.com with a link to the suspected pirated material.

We appreciate your help in protecting our authors and our ability to bring you valuable content.

Questions

If you have a problem with any aspect of this book, you can contact us at questions@packtpub.com, and we will do our best to address the problem.

1
Advanced SQL

This book is all about an open source software product, a relational database called **PostgreSQL**. PostgreSQL is an advanced SQL database server, available on a wide range of platforms. The purpose of this book is to teach database developers the fundamental practices and techniques to program database applications with PostgreSQL.

In this chapter, we will discuss the following advanced SQL topics:

- Creating views
- Understanding materialized views
- Creating cursors
- Using the GROUP BY clause
- Using the HAVING clause
- Understanding complex topics such as subqueries and joins

Creating views

A view is a virtual table based on the result set of an SQL statement. Just like a real table, a view consist of rows and columns. The fields in a view are from one or more real tables in the database. Generally speaking, a table has a set of definitions that physically stores data. A view also has a set of definitions built on top of table(s) or other view(s) that does not physically store data. The purpose of creating views is to make sure that the user does not have access to all the data and is being restricted through a view. Also, it's better to create a view if we have a query based on multiple tables so that we can use it straightaway rather than writing a whole PSQL again and again.

Database views are created using the CREATE VIEW statement. Views can be created from a single table or multiple tables, or another view.

The basic CREATEVIEW syntax is as follows:

```
CREATE VIEW view_name AS
SELECT column1, column2
FROM table_name
WHERE [condition];
```

Let's take a look at each of these commands:

- CREATE VIEW: This command helps create the database's view.
- SELECT: This command helps you select the physical and virtual columns that you want as part of the view.
- FROM: This command gives the table names with an alias from where we can fetch the columns. This may include one or more table names, considering you have to create a view at the top of multiple tables.
- WHERE: This command provides a condition that will restrict the data for a view. Also, if you include multiple tables in the FROM clause, you can provide the joining condition under the WHERE clause.

You can then query this view as though it were a table. (In PostgreSQL, at the time of writing, views are read-only by default.) You can SELECT data from a view just as you would from a table and join it to other tables; you can also use WHERE clauses. Each time you execute a SELECT query using the view, the data is rebuilt, so it is always up-to-date. It is not a frozen copy stored at the time the view was created.

Let's create a view on supplier and order tables. But, before that, let's see what the structure of the suppliers and orders table is:

```
CREATE TABLE suppliers
(supplier_id number primary key,
Supplier_name varchar(30),
Phone_number number);
CREATE TABLE orders
(order_number number primary key,
Supplier_id  number references suppliers(supplier_id),
Quanity number,
Is_active varchar(10),
Price number);
CREATE VIEW active_supplier_orders AS
SELECT suppliers.supplier_id, suppliers.supplier_name  orders.quantity,
orders.price
FROM suppliers
INNER JOIN orders
ON suppliers.supplier_id = orders.supplier_id
WHERE suppliers.supplier_name = 'XYZ COMPANY'
```

```
And orders.active='TRUE';
```

The preceding example will create a virtual table based on the result set of the SELECT statement. You can now query the PostgreSQL VIEW as follows:

```
SELECT * FROM active_supplier_orders;
```

Deleting and replacing views

To delete a view, simply use the DROP VIEW statement with view_name. The basic DROPVIEW syntax is as follows:

```
DROP VIEW IF EXISTS view_name;
```

If you want to replace an existing view with one that has the same name and returns the same set of columns, you can use a CREATE OR REPLACE command.

The following is the syntax to modify an existing view:

```
CREATE OR REPLACE VIEW view_name AS
SELECT column_name(s)
FROM table_name(s)
WHERE condition;
```

Let's take a look at each of these commands:

- CREATE OR REPLACE VIEW: This command helps modify the existing view.
- SELECT: This command selects the columns that you want as part of the view.
- FROM: This command gives the table name from where we can fetch the columns. This may include one or more table names, since you have to create a view at the top of multiple tables.
- WHERE: This command provides the condition to restrict the data for a view. Also, if you include multiple tables in the FROM clause, you can provide the joining condition under the WHERE clause.

Let's modify a view, supplier_orders, by adding some more columns in the view. The view was originally based on supplier and order tables having supplier_id, supplier_name, quantity, and price. Let's also add order_number in the view.

```
CREATE OR REPLACE VIEW active_supplier_orders AS
SELECT suppliers.supplier_id, suppliers.supplier_name  orders.quantity,
orders.price,order. order_number
FROM suppliers
```

```
INNER JOIN orders
ON suppliers.supplier_id = orders.supplier_id
WHERE suppliers.supplier_name = 'XYZ COMPANY'
And orders.active='TRUE';;
```

Materialized views

A materialized view is a table that actually contains rows but behaves like a view. This has been added in the PostgreSQL 9.3 version. A materialized view cannot subsequently be directly updated, and the query used to create the materialized view is stored in exactly the same way as the view's query is stored. As it holds the actual data, it occupies space as per the filters that we applied while creating the materialized view.

Why materialized views?

Before we get too deep into how to implement materialized views, let's first examine why we may want to use materialized views.

You may notice that certain queries are very slow. You may have exhausted all the techniques in the standard bag of techniques to speed up those queries. In the end, you will realize that getting queries to run as fast as you want simply isn't possible without completely restructuring the data.

Now, if you have an environment where you run the same type of SELECT query multiple times against the same set of tables, then you can create a materialized view for SELECT so that, on every run, this view does not go to the actual tables to fetch the data, which will obviously reduce the load on them as you might be running a **Data Manipulation Language (DML)** against your actual tables at the same time. So, basically, you take a view and turn it into a real table that holds real data rather than a gateway to a SELECT query.

Read-only, updatable, and writeable materialized views

A materialized view can be read-only, updatable, or writeable. Users cannot perform DML statements on read-only materialized views, but they can perform them on updatable and writeable materialized views.

Read-only materialized views

You can make a materialized view read-only during creation by omitting the FOR UPDATE clause or by disabling the equivalent option in the database management tool. Read-only materialized views use many mechanisms similar to updatable materialized views, except they do not need to belong to a materialized view group.

In a replication environment, a materialized table holds the table data and resides in a different database. A table that has a materialized view on it is called a master table. The master table resides on a master site and the materialized view resides on a materialized-view site.

In addition, using read-only materialized views eliminates the possibility of introducing data conflicts on the master site or the master materialized view site, although this convenience means that updates cannot be made on the remote materialized view site.

The syntax to create a materialized view is as follows:

```
CREATE MATERIALIZED VIEW  view_name AS SELECT  columns FROM table;
```

The CREATE MATERIALIZED VIEW command helps us create a materialized view. The command acts in way similar to the CREATE VIEW command, which was explained in the previous section.

Let's make a read-only materialized view for a supplier table:

```
CREATE MATERIALIZED VIEW suppliers_matview AS
SELECT * FROM suppliers;
```

This view is a read-only materialized view and will not reflect the changes to the master site.

Updatable materialized views

You can make a materialized view updatable during creation by including the FOR UPDATE clause or enabling the equivalent option in the database management tool. In order for changes that have been made to an updatable materialized view to be reflected in the master site during refresh, the updatable materialized view must belong to a materialized view group.

When we say "refreshing the materialized view," we mean synchronizing the data in the materialized view with data in its master table.

An updatable materialized view enables you to decrease the load on master sites because users can make changes to data on the materialized view site.

The syntax to create an updatable materialized view is as follows:

```
CREATE MATERIALIZED VIEW  view_name  FOR UPDATE
AS
SELECT columns FROM table;
```

Let's make an updatable materialized view for a supplier table:

```
CREATE MATERIALIZED VIEW suppliers_matview FOR UPDATE
AS
SELECT * FROM suppliers;
```

Whenever changes are made in the `suppliers_matview` clause, it will reflect the changes to the master sites during refresh.

Writeable materialized views

A writeable materialized view is one that is created using the `FOR UPDATE` clause like an updatable materialized view is, but it is not a part of a materialized view group. Users can perform DML operations on a writeable materialized view; however, if you refresh the materialized view, then these changes are not pushed back to the master site and are lost in the materialized view itself. Writeable materialized views are typically allowed wherever fast-refreshable, read-only materialized views are allowed.

Creating cursors

A cursor in PostgreSQL is a read-only pointer to a fully executed `SELECT` statement's result set. Cursors are typically used within applications that maintain a persistent connection to the PostgreSQL backend. By executing a cursor and maintaining a reference to its returned result set, an application can more efficiently manage which rows to retrieve from a result set at different times without re-executing the query with different `LIMIT` and `OFFSET` clauses.

The four SQL commands involved with PostgreSQL cursors are `DECLARE`, `FETCH`, `MOVE`, and `CLOSE`.

The DECLARE command both defines and opens a cursor, in effect defining the cursor in memory, and then populates the cursor with information about the result set returned from the executed query. A cursor may be declared only within an existing transaction block, so you must execute a BEGIN command prior to declaring a cursor.

Here is the syntax for DECLARE:

```
DECLARE cursorname [ BINARY ] [ INSENSITIVE ] [ SCROLL ] CURSOR  FOR query
[ FOR { READ ONLY | UPDATE [ OF  column [, ...] ] } ]
```

DECLARE cursorname is the name of the cursor to create. The optional BINARY keyword causes the output to be retrieved in binary format instead of standard ASCII; this can be more efficient, though it is only relevant to custom applications as clients such as **psql** are not built to handle anything but text output. The INSENSITIVE and SCROLL keywords exist to comply with the SQL standard, though they each define PostgreSQL's default behavior and are never necessary. The INSENSITIVE SQL keyword exists to ensure that all data retrieved from the cursor remains unchanged from other cursors or connections. As PostgreSQL requires the cursors to be defined within transaction blocks, this behavior is already implied. The SCROLL SQL keyword exists to specify that multiple rows at a time can be selected from the cursor. This is the default in PostgreSQL, even if it is unspecified.

The CURSOR FOR query is the complete query and its result set will be accessible by the cursor when executed.

The [FOR { READ ONLY | UPDATE [OF column [, ...]] }] cursors may only be defined as READ ONLY, and the FOR clause is, therefore, superfluous.

Let's begin a transaction block with the BEGIN keyword, and open a cursor named order_cur with SELECT * FROM orders as its executed select statement:

```
BEGIN;
DECLARE order_cur CURSOR
FOR SELECT * FROM orders;
```

Once the cursor is successfully declared, it means that the rows retrieved by the query are now accessible from the order_cur cursor.

Using cursors

In order to retrieve rows from the open cursor, we need to use the FETCH command. The MOVE command moves the current location of the cursor within the result set and the CLOSE command closes the cursor, freeing up any associated memory.

Here is the syntax for the FETCH SQL command:

```
FETCH [ FORWARD | BACKWARD]
[ # | ALL | NEXT | PRIOR ]
{ IN | FROM }
cursor
```

cursor is the name of the cursor from where we can retrieve row data. A cursor always points to a current position in the executed statement's result set and rows can be retrieved either ahead of the current location or behind it. The FORWARD and BACKWARD keywords may be used to specify the direction, though the default is forward. The NEXT keyword (the default) returns the next single row from the current cursor position. The PRIOR keyword causes the single row preceding the current cursor position to be returned.

Let's consider an example that fetches the first four rows stored in the result set, pointed to by the order_cur cursor. As a direction is not specified, FORWARD is implied. It then uses a FETCH statement with the NEXT keyword to select the fifth row, and then another FETCH statement with the PRIOR keyword to again select the fourth retrieved row.

```
FETCH 4 FROM order_cur;
```

In this case, the first four rows will be fetched.

Closing a cursor

You can use the CLOSE command to explicitly close an open cursor. A cursor can also be implicitly closed if the transaction block that it resides within is committed with the COMMIT command, or rolled back with the ROLLBACK command.

Here is the syntax for the CLOSE command, where Cursorname is the name of the cursor intended to be closed:

```
CLOSE
Cursorname;
```

Using the GROUP BY clause

The GROUP BY clause enables you to establish data groups based on columns. The grouping criterion is defined by the GROUP BY clause, which is followed by the WHERE clause in the SQL execution path. Following this execution path, the result set rows are grouped based on like values of grouping columns and the WHERE clause restricts the entries in each group.

All columns that are used besides the aggregate functions must be included in the GROUP BY clause. The GROUP BY clause does not support the use of column aliases; you must use the actual column names. The GROUP BY columns may or may not appear in the SELECT list. The GROUP BY clause can only be used with aggregate functions such as SUM, AVG, COUNT, MAX, and MIN.

The following statement illustrates the syntax of the GROUP BY clause:

```
SELECT expression1, expression2, ... expression_n,
aggregate_function (expression)
FROM tables
WHERE conditions
GROUP BY expression1, expression2, ... expression_n;
```

The expression1, expression2, ... expression_n commands are expressions that are not encapsulated within an aggregate function and must be included in the GROUP BY clause.

Let's take a look at these commands:

- aggregate_function: This performs many functions, such as SUM (http://www.techonthenet.com/oracle/functions/sum.php), COUNT (http://www.techonthenet.com/oracle/functions/count.php), MIN (http://www.techonthenet.com/oracle/functions/min.php), MAX (http://www.techonthenet.com/oracle/functions/max.php), or AVG (http://www.techonthenet.com/oracle/functions/avg.php).
- tables: This is where you can retrieve records from. There must be at least one table listed in the FROM clause.
- conditions: This is a condition that must be met for the records to be selected.

The GROUP BY clause must appear right after the FROM or WHERE clause. Followed by the GROUP BY clause is one column or a list of comma-separated columns. You can also put an expression in the GROUP BY clause.

As mentioned in the previous paragraph, the GROUP BY clause divides rows returned from the SELECT statement into groups. For each group, you can apply an aggregate function, for example, to calculate the sum of items or count the number of items in the groups.

Let's look at a GROUP BY query example that uses the SUM function (http://www.techonthe
net.com/oracle/functions/sum.php). This example uses the SUM function to return the
name of the product and the total sales (for the product).

```
SELECT product, SUM(sale) AS "Total sales"
FROM order_details
GROUP BY product;
```

In the select statement, we have sales where we applied the SUM function and the other field
product is not part of SUM, we must use in the GROUP BY clause.

Using the HAVING clause

In the previous section, we discussed about GROUP BY clause, however if you want to
restrict the groups of returned rows, you can use HAVING clause. The HAVING clause is used
to specify which individual group(s) is to be displayed, or in simple language we use the
HAVING clause in order to filter the groups on the basis of an aggregate function condition.

Note: The WHERE clause cannot be used to return the desired groups. The WHERE clause is
only used to restrict individual rows. When the GROUP BY clause is not used, the HAVING
clause works like the WHERE clause.

The syntax for the PostgreSQL HAVING clause is as follows:

```
SELECT expression1, expression2, ... expression_n,
aggregate_function (expression)
FROM tables
WHERE conditions
GROUP BY expression1, expression2, ... expression_n
HAVING group_condition;
```

Parameters or arguments

aggregate_function can be a function such as SUM, COUNT, MIN, MAX, or AVG.

expression1, expression2, ... expression_n are expressions that are not
encapsulated within an aggregate function and must be included in the GROUP BY clause.

conditions are the conditions used to restrict the groups of returned rows. Only those
groups whose condition evaluates to true will be included in the result set.

Let's consider an example where you try to fetch the product that has `sales>10000`:

```
SELECT product, SUM(sale) AS "Total sales"
FROM order_details
GROUP BY product
Having sum(sales)>10000;
```

The PostgreSQL `HAVING` clause will filter the results so that only the total sales greater than `10000` will be returned.

Using the UPDATE operation clauses

The PostgreSQL `UPDATE` query is used to modify the existing records in a table. You can use the `WHERE` clause with the `UPDATE` query to update selected rows; otherwise, all the rows will be updated.

The basic syntax of the `UPDATE` query with the `WHERE` clause is as follows:

```
UPDATE table_name
SET column1 = value1, column2 = value2...., columnN = valueN
WHERE [condition];
```

You can combine *n* number of conditions using the `AND` or `OR` operators.

The following is an example that will update `SALARY` for an employee whose `ID` is 6:

```
UPDATE employee SET SALARY = 15000 WHERE ID = 6;
```

This will update the salary to `15000` whose `ID` = `6`.

Using the LIMIT clause

The `LIMIT` clause is used to retrieve a number of rows from a larger data set. It helps fetch the top *n* records. The `LIMIT` and `OFFSET` clauses allow you to retrieve just a portion of the rows that are generated by the rest of the query from a result set:

```
SELECT select_list
FROM table_expression
[LIMIT { number | ALL }] [OFFSET number]
```

If a limit count is given, no more than that many rows will be returned (but possibly fewer, if the query itself yields fewer rows). LIMIT ALL is the same as omitting the LIMIT clause.

The OFFSET clause suggests skipping many rows before beginning to return rows. OFFSET 0 is the same as omitting the OFFSET clause. If both OFFSET and LIMIT appear, then the OFFSET rows will be skipped before starting to count the LIMIT rows that are returned.

Using subqueries

A subquery is a query within a query. In other words, a subquery is a SQL query nested inside a larger query. It may occur in a SELECT, FROM, or WHERE clause. In PostgreSQL, a subquery can be nested inside a SELECT, INSERT, UPDATE, DELETE, SET, or DO statement or inside another subquery. It is usually added within the WHERE clause of another SQL SELECT statement. You can use comparison operators, such as >, <, or =. Comparison operators can also be a multiple-row operator, such as IN, ANY, SOME, or ALL. It can be treated as an inner query that is an SQL query placed as a part of another query called as outer query. The inner query is executed before its parent query so that the results of the inner query can be passed to the outer query.

The following statement illustrates the subquery syntax:

```
SELECT column list
FROM table
WHERE table.columnname expr_operator
(SELECT column FROM table)
```

The query inside the brackets is called the inner query. The query that contains the subquery is called the outer query.

PostgreSQL executes the query that contains a subquery in the following sequence:

- First, it executes the subquery
- Second, it gets the results and passes it to the outer query
- Third, it executes the outer query

Let's consider an example where you want to find employee_id, first_name, last_name, and salary for employees whose salary is higher than the average salary throughout the company.

We can do this in two steps:

1. First, find the average salary from the `employee` table.
2. Then, use the answer in the second `SELECT` statement to find employees who have a higher `salary` from the result (which is the average salary).

```
SELECT avg(salary) from employee;
Result: 25000
SELECT employee_id,first_name,last_name,salary
FROM employee
WHERE salary > 25000;
```

This does seem rather inelegant. What we really want to do is pass the result of the first query straight into the second query without needing to remember it, and type it back for a second query.

The solution is to use a subquery. We put the first query in brackets, and use it as part of

a `WHERE` clause to the second query, as follows:

```
SELECT employee_id,first_name,last_name,salary
FROM employee
WHERE salary > (Select avg(salary) from employee);
```

PostgreSQL runs the query in brackets first, that is, the average of salary. After getting the answer, it then runs the outer query, substituting the answer from the inner query, and tries to find the employees whose `salary` is higher than the average.

> Note: A subquery that returns exactly one column value from one row is called a **scalar subquery**. The `SELECT` query is executed and the single returned value is used in the surrounding value expression. It is an error to use a query that returns more than one row or column as a scalar subquery. If the subquery returns no rows during a particular execution, it is not an error, and the scalar result is taken to be null. The subquery can refer to variables from the surrounding query, which will act as constants during any one evaluation of the subquery.

Subqueries that return multiple rows

In the previous section, we saw subqueries that only returned a single result because an aggregate function was used in the subquery. Subqueries can also return zero or more rows.

Subqueries that return multiple rows can be used with the ALL, IN, ANY, or SOME operators. We can also negate the condition like NOT IN.

Correlated subqueries

A subquery that references one or more columns from its containing SQL statement is called a correlated subquery. Unlike non-correlated subqueries that are executed exactly once prior to the execution of a containing statement, a correlated subquery is executed once for each candidate row in the intermediate result set of the containing query.

The following statement illustrates the syntax of a correlated subquery:

```
SELECT column1,column2,..
FROM table 1 outer
WHERE column1 operator( SELECT column1 from table 2 WHERE
column2=outer.column4)
```

The PostgreSQL runs will pass the value of `column4` from the outer table to the inner query and will be compared to `column2` of `table 2`. Accordingly, `column1` will be fetched from `table 2` and depending on the operator it will be compared to `column1` of the outer table. If the expression turned out to be true, the row will be passed; otherwise, it will not appear in the output.

But with the correlated queries you might see some performance issues. This is because of the fact that for every record of the outer query, the correlated subquery will be executed. The performance is completely dependent on the data involved. However, in order to make sure that the query works efficiently, we can use some temporary tables.

Let's try to find all the employees who earn more than the average salary in their department:

```
SELECT last_name, salary, department_id
FROM employee outer
WHERE salary >
(SELECT AVG(salary)
FROM employee
WHERE department_id = outer.department_id);
```

For each row from the `employee` table, the value of `department_id` will be passed into the inner query (let's consider that the value of `department_id` of the first row is 30) and the inner query will try to find the average salary of that particular `department_id` = 30. If the salary of that particular record will be more than the average salary of `department_id` = 30, the expression will turn out to be true and the record will come in the output.

Existence subqueries

The PostgreSQL `EXISTS` condition is used in combination with a subquery, and is considered to be met if the subquery returns at least one row. It can be used in a `SELECT`, `INSERT`, `UPDATE`, or `DELETE` statement. If a subquery returns any rows at all, the `EXISTS` subquery is true, and the `NOT EXISTS` subquery is false.

The syntax for the PostgreSQL `EXISTS` condition is as follows:

```
WHERE EXISTS ( subquery );
```

Parameters or arguments

The `subquery` is a `SELECT` statement that usually starts with `SELECT *` rather than a list of expressions or column names. To increase performance, you could replace `SELECT *` with `SELECT 1` as the column result of the subquery is not relevant (only the rows returned matter).

> The SQL statements that use the `EXISTS` condition in PostgreSQL are very inefficient as the subquery is re-run for every row in the outer query's table. There are more efficient ways, such as using joins to write most queries, that do not use the `EXISTS` condition.

Let's look at the following example that is a `SELECT` statement and uses the PostgreSQL `EXISTS` condition:

```
SELECT * FROM products
WHERE EXISTS (SELECT 1
FROM inventory
WHERE products.product_id = inventory.product_id);
```

This PostgreSQL EXISTS condition example will return all records from the products table where there is at least one record in the inventory table with the matching product_id. We used SELECT 1 in the subquery to increase performance as the column result set is not relevant to the EXISTS condition (only the existence of a returned row matters).

The PostgreSQL EXISTS condition can also be combined with the NOT operator, for example:

```
SELECT * FROM products
WHERE NOT EXISTS (SELECT 1
FROM inventory
WHERE products.product_id = inventory.product_id);
```

This PostgreSQL NOT EXISTS example will return all records from the products table where there are no records in the inventory table for the given product_id.

Using the Union join

The PostgreSQL UNION clause is used to combine the results of two or more SELECT statements without returning any duplicate rows.

The basic rules to combine two or more queries using the UNION join are as follows:

- The number and order of columns of all queries must be the same
- The data types of the columns on involving table in each query must be same or compatible
- Usually, the returned column names are taken from the first query

By default, the UNION join behaves like DISTINCT, that is, eliminates the duplicate rows; however, using the ALL keyword with the UNION join returns all rows, including the duplicates, as shown in the following example:

```
SELECT <column_list>
FROM   table
WHERE  condition
GROUP BY  <column_list>  [HAVING ] condition
UNION
SELECT <column_list>
FROM   table
WHERE  condition
GROUP BY  <column_list>  [HAVING ] condition
ORDER BY column list;
```

The queries are all executed independently, but their output is merged. The Union operator may place rows in the first query, before, after, or in between the rows in the result set of the second query. To sort the records in a combined result set, you can use ORDER BY.

Let's consider an example where you combine the data of customers belonging to two different sites. The table structure of both the tables is the same, but they have data of the customers from two different sites:

```
SELECT customer_id,customer_name,location_id
FROM   customer_site1
UNION
SELECT customer_id,customer_name,location_id
FROM   customer_site2
ORDER BY customer_name  asc;
```

Both the SELECT queries would run individually, combine the result set, remove the duplicates (as we are using UNION), and sort the result set according to the condition, which is customer_name in this case.

Using the Self join

The tables we are joining don't have to be different ones. We can join a table with itself. This is called a self join. In this case, we will use aliases for the table; otherwise, PostgreSQL will not know which column of which table instance we mean. To join a table with itself means that each row of the table is combined with itself, and with every other row of the table. The self join can be viewed as a joining of two copies of the same table. The table is not actually copied but SQL carries out the command as though it were.

The syntax of the command to join a table with itself is almost the same as that of joining two different tables:

```
SELECT a.column_name, b.column_name...
FROM table1 a, table1 b
WHERE condition1 and/or condition2
```

To distinguish the column names from one another, aliases for the actual table names are used as both the tables have the same name. Table name aliases are defined in the FROM clause of the SELECT statement.

Let's consider an example where you want to find a list of employees and their supervisor. For this example, we will consider the **Employee** table that has the columns **Employee_id**, **Employee_name**, and **Supervisor_id**. The **Supervisor_id** contains nothing but the **Employee_id** of the person who the employee reports to.

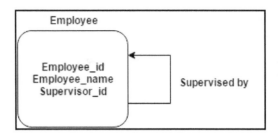

In the following example, we will use the table **Employee** twice; and in order to do this, we will use the alias of the table:

```
SELECT a.emp_id AS "Emp_ID", a.emp_name AS "Employee Name",
b.emp_id AS "Supervisor ID",b.emp_name AS "Supervisor Name"
FROM employee a, employee b
WHERE a.supervisor_id = b.emp_id;
```

For every record, it will compare the **Supervisor_id** to the **Employee_id** and the **Employee_name** to the supervisor name.

Using the Outer join

Another class of join is known as the OUTER JOIN. In OUTER JOIN, the results might contain both matched and unmatched rows. It is for this reason that beginners might find such joins a little confusing. However, the logic is really quite straightforward.

The following are the three types of Outer joins:

- The PostgreSQL LEFT OUTER JOIN (or sometimes called LEFT JOIN)
- The PostgreSQL RIGHT OUTER JOIN (or sometimes called RIGHT JOIN)
- The PostgreSQL FULL OUTER JOIN (or sometimes called FULL JOIN)

Left outer join

Left outer join returns all rows from the left-hand table specified in the ON condition, and only those rows from the other tables where the joined fields are equal (the join condition is met). If the condition is not met, the values of the columns in the second table are replaced by null values.

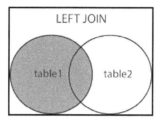

The syntax for the PostgreSQL LEFT OUTER JOIN is:

```
SELECT columns
FROM table1
LEFT OUTER JOIN table2
ON condition1, condition2
```

In the case of LEFT OUTER JOIN, an inner join is performed first. Then, for each row in table1 that does not satisfy the join condition with any row in table2, a joined row is added with null values in the columns of table2. Thus, the joined table always has at least one row for each row in table1.

Let's consider an example where you want to fetch the order details placed by a customer. Now, there can be a scenario where a customer doesn't have any order placed that is open, and the order table contains only those orders that are open. In this case, we will use a left outer join to get information on all the customers and their corresponding orders:

```
SELECT customer.customer_id, customer.customer_name, orders.order_number
FROM customer
LEFT OUTER JOIN orders
ON customer.customer_id = orders.customer_id
```

This LEFT OUTER JOIN example will return all rows from the customer table and only those rows from the orders table where the join condition is met.

If a customer_id value in the customer table does not exist in the orders table, all fields in the orders table will display as <null> in the result set.

Right outer join

Another type of join is called a PostgreSQL RIGHT OUTER JOIN. This type of join returns all rows from the right-hand table specified in the ON condition, and only those rows from the other table where the joined fields are equal (join condition is met). If the condition is not met, the value of the columns in the first table is replaced by null values.

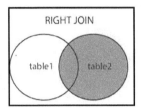

The syntax for the PostgreSQL RIGHT OUTER JOIN is as follows:

```
SELECT columns
FROM table1
RIGHT OUTER JOIN table2
ON table1.column = table2.column;
Condition1, condition2;
```

In the case of RIGHT OUTER JOIN, an inner join is performed first. Then, for each row in table2 that does not satisfy the join condition with any row in table1, a joined row is added with null values in the columns of table1. This is the converse of a left join; the result table will always have a row for each row in table2.

Let's consider an example where you want to fetch the invoice information for the orders. Now, when an order is completed, we generate an invoice for the customer so that he can pay the amount. There can be a scenario where the order has not been completed, so the invoice is not generated yet. In this case, we will use a right outer to get all the orders information and corresponding invoice information.

```
SELECT invoice.invoice_id, invoice.invoice_date,  orders.order_number
FROM invoice
RIGHT OUTER JOIN orders
ON invoice.order_number= orders.order_number
```

This RIGHT OUTER JOIN example will return all rows from the order table and only those rows from the invoice table where the joined fields are equal. If an order_number value in the invoice table does not exist, all the fields in the invoice table will display as <null> in the result set.

Full outer join

Another type of join is called a PostgreSQL FULL OUTER JOIN. This type of join returns all rows from the left-hand table and right-hand table with nulls in place where the join condition is not met.

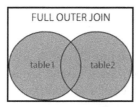

The syntax for the PostgreSQL FULL OUTER JOIN is as follows:

```
SELECT columns
FROM table1
FULL OUTER JOIN table2
ON table1.column = table2.column;
Condition1,condition2;
```

First, an inner join is performed. Then, for each row in table1 that does not satisfy the join condition with any row in table2, a joined row is added with null values in the columns of table2. Also, for each row of table2 that does not satisfy the join condition with any row in table1, a joined row with null values in the columns of table1 is added.

Let's consider an example where you want to fetch an invoice information and all the orders information. In this case, we will use a full outer to get all the orders information and the corresponding invoice information.

```
SELECT invoice.invoice_id, invoice.invoice_date, orders.order_number
FROM invoice
FULL  OUTER JOIN orders
ON invoice.order_number= orders.order_number;
```

This FULL OUTER JOIN example will return all rows from the invoice table and the orders table and, whenever the join condition is not met, <null> will be extended to those fields in the result set.

If an `order_number` value in the `invoice` table does not exist in the `orders` table, all the fields in the `orders` table will display as `<null>` in the result set. If order number in order's table does not exist in the `invoice` table, all fields in the `invoice` table will display as `<null>` in the result set.

Summary

After reading this chapter, you will be familiar with advanced concepts of PostgreSQL. We talked about views and materialized views, which are really significant. We also talked about cursors that help run a few rows at a time rather than full query at once. This helps avoid memory overrun when results contain a large number of rows. Another usage is to return a reference to a cursor that a function has created and allow the caller to read the rows. In addition to these, we discussed the aggregation concept by using the GROUP BY clause, which is really important for calculations. Another topic that we discussed in this chapter is subquery, which is a powerful feature of PostgreSQL. However, subqueries that contain an outer reference can be very inefficient. In many instances, these queries can be rewritten to remove the outer reference, which can improve performance. Other than that, the concept we covered is join, along with self, union, and outer join; these are really helpful when we need data from multiple tables. In the next chapter, we will discuss conversion between the data types and how to deal with arrays. Also we will talk about some complex data types, such as JSON and XML.

2
Data Manipulation

In the previous chapter, we talked about some advanced concepts of PostgreSQL such as views, materialized views, cursors, and some complex topics such as subqueries and joins. In this chapter, we will discuss the basics that will help you understand how data manipulation of datatypes is done in PostgreSQL and how to manage and use arrays with the help of examples. Additionally, we will cover how to manage XML and JSON data. At the end of the chapter, we will discuss the usage of composite datatype.

Conversion between datatypes

Like other languages, PostgreSQL has one of the significant features, that is, conversion of datatypes. Many times, we will need to convert between datatypes in a database. Type conversions are very useful, and sometimes necessary, while running queries. For example, we are trying to import data from another system and the target-column datatype is different from the source-column datatype; we can use the conversion feature of PostgreSQL to implement runtime conversions between compatible datatypes using CAST functions. The following is the syntax:

```
CAST ( expression AS type )
```

Or

```
expression :: type
```

This contains a column name or a literal for which you want to convert the datatype. Converting null values returns nulls. The expression cannot contain blank or empty strings. The type-datatype to which you want to convert the expression.

Let's consider an example of an `order` table where we want to change the date type to a character.

```
SELECT cast(ordered_date AS char(10)) FROM order;
```

In the preceding example, we are converting `ordered_date`, having datatype as a date for character datatype.

Also, we can use `::` to do the same:

```
SELECT ordered_date:: char(10) FROM order;
```

`pg_cast` stores datatype conversion paths that are built-in and the one that is being defined with the help of `CREATE CAST`:

```
SELECT castsource::regtype, casttarget::regtype FROM pg_cast limit 2;
castsource | casttarget
-----------+-----------
bigint     | smallint
bigint     | integer
(2 rows)
```

Introduction to arrays

PostgreSQL supports columns to defined as an array. This array is of a variable length and can be defined as a one-dimensional or multidimensional array. You can create an array of any datatype, such as text, integer, or composite type, by appending `[]` at the end of the type. For example, you can declare an array of an integer type by using `int[]` or character data by using `text[]`. This array support in PostgreSQL helps build aggregate functions using `IN` and `ANY` clauses. We will explore its use in a later section.

Array constructors

An array can be created with the help of an `ARRAY` keyword comprising the list of expressions enclosed in square brackets:

```
SELECT ARRAY[1,2,3] AS sample_array;
Output
Sample_array
------- --------- ---
{1,2,3}
```

By default, the datatype of the preceding array will be an integer as it is the common datatype for all members of `sample_array`. You can explicitly override the array datatype to the other datatype by using the array constructor, for example:

```
SELECT ARRAY[1,2,3.2] :: integer[] AS sample_array;
Sample_array
------- ---------- ---
{1,2,3}
```

We can also define the array while defining the table and after that we can insert the data in it.

Let's create a `supplier` table that has a `product` column:

```
CREATE TABLE supplier
(name text, product  text[])
```

In the preceding example, we created a table `supplier` with a `text`-type column for the name of the supplier, and a column `product` that represents the names of products having a one-dimensional array.

Now, let's insert data in the preceding table and see how it looks:

```
INSERT INTO supplier
VALUES
('Supplier1','{ "table","chair","desk" }' )
```

We should use double quotes while inserting the members as the single quotes give an error:

```
SELECT * FROM supplier;

Output
name        |          members
----------+----------------------------
Supplier1 | {table,chair,desk}
(1 row)
```

We can insert the data using the array constructor as well:

```
INSERT INTO supplier
VALUES
(' Supplier2 ', ARRAY['pen','page '] )
```

While using the array constructor, the values can be inserted using single quotes:

```
SELECT * FROM supplier;

Output:
name       |       members
-----------+--------------------------
Supplier1 | {table,chair,desk}
Supplier2 | {pen,page}
```

We can also get the values from another query and straightaway put them in an array.

Let's take an example where we want to put all the products in a single row. We have a product table that has product_id and product_name as columns. This can be done with the help of the function array().

```
SELECT array(SELECT distinct product_name FROM supplier WHERE
name='Supplier1') AS product_name;
Output
Product_name
---- ---- ----- -----
{table,chair, desk}
```

In the previous example, the inner query will fetch the distinct values of products whereas the outer one will convert these into an array.

As discussed earlier, PostgreSQL supports multidimensional arrays as well. Let's consider an example to see how it works. Let's declare a table supplier that has a product_category column as a one-dimensional array and its product as a two-dimensional array:

```
CREATE TABLE supplier (
name text,
product_category text[],
product text[][]
);
```

Now, let's see how to insert the data in a two-dimensional array:

```
INSERT INTO supplier
  VALUES ('Supplier1', '{"Stationary","Books"}',
  '{{"Pen", "Pencil"}, {"PostgreSqlCookBook", "Oracle Performance"}}');

INSERT INTO supplier
  VALUES ('Supplier2', '{"LivingRoom Furniture"," Dinning Furniture"}',
  '{{"Sofa", "Table"}, {"Chair", "Cabinet"}}');
```

Since we have inserted the data in the two-dimensional array, let's query the `supplier` table and check how the data looks:

```
SELECT * FROM supplier;

name        |       product_category       |                product
------------+------------------------------+--------------------------------
Supplier1   | {Stationary,Books}           | {{Pen, Pencil} {PostgreSqlCookBook,
Oracle Performance}}
Supplier2   | {LivingRoomFurniture,Dinning Furniture} | {{Sofa, Table}
{Chair, Cabinet}}
```

In multidimensional arrays, extends of each dimension should match. A mismatch causes an error, for example: `ERROR: multidimensional arrays must have array expressions with matching dimensions`.

A huge variety of array functions, are available in PostgreSQL. Let's discuss a couple of them.

String_to_array()

PostgreSQL supports many array functions, one of which, is the `string_to_array` function. As the name states, this function helps convert the string into an array.

The following is the syntax for this function:

```
String_To_Array(String,delimeter)
```

- **String**: This is the value that we need to convert to the array
- **Delimeter**: This will help you tell how the string needs to be converted to an array

Let's take an example in which we have a string that we will convert into an array:

```
SELECT string_to_array ('This is a sample string to be converted into an
array',' ');
Output
String_to_array
--- ---- ----- ----- ----
{This,is,a,sample,string,to,be,converted,into,an,array}
```

In the preceding example, we have taken delimeter as space so all the words that have a space in between will be considered as individual members of the array.You can always go back and convert the array into a string using the other function `array_to_string`, which works in a similar manner.

Here is an example to convert an array into a string:

```
SELECT array_to_string (ARRAY[1, 2, 3], ',');
Output
array_to_string
----------------
1,2,3
```

Array_dims( )

We can check the dimensions of an array using the `array_dims` function. It will help us know the number of values stored in an array. The following is the syntax:

```
Array_dims(column_name)
```

Let's take an example:

```
SELECT array_dims (product_category) FROM supplier;
Output
array_dims
------------
 [1:2]
 [1:2]
(2 rows)
```

Another example for a multidimensional array is as follows:

```
SELECT array_dims (product) FROM supplier;
Output
array_dims
------------
 [1:2] [1:2]
 [1:2] [1:2]
```

ARRAY_AGG()

The `ARRAY_AGG` function is used to concatenate values including null into an array. Let's consider an example to see how it works:

```
SELECT name FROM supplier;
name
----|----
Supplier1
Supplier2
(2 rows)
```

Now, suppose, based on the preceding table, you want to use the ARRAY_AGG function; you can do so using the following command:

```
SELECT ARRAY_AGG(NAME) FROM supplier;

Output:
array_agg
------------------------------------------------
 {Supplier1,Supplier2}
```

The array_agg returns NULL value instead of an empty array when there is no input rows. Considering we have a blank record in supplier table like following:

```
SELECT name FROM supplier;
name
----|--

Supplier1
Supplier2
(3 rows)
```

When we use array_agg, the output will look like this:

```
SELECT ARRAY_AGG(NAME) FROM supplier;
Output:
array_agg
-------------------------------------------------
 {Supplier2,Supplier1,NULL}
```

We can use the array_to_string function as well in order to ignore NULL:

```
SELECT array_to_string(array_agg(name), ',') FROM supplier;
array_to_string
-----------------
 Supplier2,Supplier1
```

In version 9.x, we can use COALESCE in order to handle a null or an empty array:

```
SELECT array_to_string(array_agg(coalesce(name, '')), ',') FROM supplier;
array_to_string
-----------------
 Supplier2,Supplier1
```

ARRAY_UPPER()

The ARRAY_UPPER() function returns the upper bound of the array dimension. The following is the syntax for the same:

```
array_upper(anyarray, int)
```

- **Anyarray**: This is the array column name or the array for which you want the upper bound

It will return the integer. The following is an example:

```
SELECT array_upper(product,1) FROM supplier WHERE name='Supplier1';

Array_upper
----------
2
```

Similarly, we can use the ARRAY_LOWER() function to check the lower bound of the array.

Array_length()

This function returns the length of the requested array. The following is the syntax:

```
array_length(anyarray, int)
```

- **Anyarray**: This is the array column name or the array for which you want the upper bound

It will return the integer. The following is an example:

```
SELECT array_length(product,1) FROM supplier WHERE name='Supplier1';

Array_length
----------
2
```

Array slicing and splicing

PostgreSQL supports slicing an array, which can be done by providing the start and end of the array or the lower bound and upper bound of an array. It will be a subset of the array that you are trying to slice.

The following is the syntax:

```
lower-bound:upper-bound
```

Let's try to slice an array using the preceding syntax:

```
SELECT product_category[1:1] FROM supplier;

product_category
-------+-----------------
{Stationary}
 {LivingRoom Furniture}
```

We can also write the preceding query as follows:

```
SELECT product_category[1] FROM supplier;
```

If any of the subscripts are written in the `lower:upper` form, they are considered to be slices. If only one value is specified in the subscript, then, by default, the value of the lower bound is 1, which means `product_category[2]` is considered as `[1:2]`.

```
SELECT product[1:2][2] FROM supplier;
product
-------+------------------------------- +-------------------------------
------
{{Pen, Pencil}, {PostgreSqlCookBook, Oracle Performance}}
```

UNNESTing arrays to rows

PostgreSql supports a function that helps in expanding the array to rows, which means that you can expand the elements of the array to an individual record. This can be done with the help of `unnest`. Unnest can be used with multidimensional arrays as well.

The following is the syntax:

```
unnest(anyarray)
```

Let's take an example where we have the following content:

```
Product_category | product
------------------|-----------
Furniture         |chair,table,desk
Stationary        |pencil,pen,book

SELECT Product_category, unnest(string_to_array(product, ',')) AS product
FROM supplier;
```

```
Product_category | product
-----------------|-----------
Furniture        |chair
Furniture        |table
Furniture        |desk
Stationary       |pencil
Stationary       |pen
Stationary       |book
```

You can also directly put members of the array using the array syntax and then use `unnest`:

```
SELECT unnest(array[chair,table,desk]);
unnest
--------
chair
table
desk
(3 rows)
```

Also, PostgreSQL supports a multi-argument `unnest` as well. It behaves in the same way as a table using multiple `unnest` calls.

Let's take an example:

```
SELECT * FROM unnest(array[a,b],array[c,d,e]);
unnest | unnest
-------+--------
a      | c
b      | d
Null   | e
```

In the preceding example, we get a NULL value in the output because the array contains fewer values than some other array in the same table clause.

To use unnest with multiple arguments, you will need to make sure that the unnest is used in the FROM clause rather than the SELECT clause, otherwise it will throw an error.

```
SELECT unnest(array[a,b],array[c,d,e]);
ERROR: function unnest(integer[], integer[]) does not exist
LINE 1: SELECT unnest(array[a,b],array[c,d,e]);
```

Introduction to JSON

PostgreSQL supports the JSON datatype, which is useful to store multilevel, dynamically structured object graphs. Although the data can be stored in text, the JSON datatype verifies whether the value is in valid JSON format. There are two JSON datatypes: `json` and `jsonb`. Although they accept the same values as input, they have difference in their efficiency. Indexing is supported by `jsonb`.

 The `json` datatype stores data as such due to which it has to reparse while execution. The `jsonb` datatype stores in binary format, which it converts during conversion, but it doesn't reparse during execution, so it is faster in comparison to `json`.

Inserting JSON data in PostgreSQL

Let's create a table first in which we will have only two columns—`id` and `data`:

```
CREATE TABLE product_info (id serial, data jsonb);
```

Once the table is created, let's insert some data in it:

```
INSERT INTO product_info (data) VALUES
('{"product_name":"chair","product_category":"Furniture","price":"200"}'),
('{"product_name":"table","product_category":"Furniture","price":"500"}'),
('{"product_name":"pen","product_category":"Stationary","price":"100"}'),
('{"product_name":"pencil","product_category":"
Stationary","price":"50"}');
```

Now, let's see how the data looks:

```
SELECT * FROM product_info;
id  |                     data
----+-------------------------------------------
  1 | {"product_name":"chair","product_category":"Furniture","price":"200"}
  2 | {"product_name":"table","product_category":"Furniture","price":"500"}
  3 | {"product_name":"pen","product_category":"Stationary","price":"100"}
  4 | {"product_name":"pencil","product_category":"
Stationary","price":"50"}
```

Querying JSON

Whenever we develop a query to get a result, we will always use the comparison operator to filter data.

Equality operation

This is only available for `jsonb`; we can get two JSON objects that are identical:

```
SELECT * FROM product_info WHERE data =
'{"product_category":"Stationary"}';
id  |    data
----+---------------------------------------------------------------
 (0 rows)
```

We got zero records because we don't have any record equal to `product_category:Stationary`.

Containment

Containment means **is a subset of**. We can query if one JSON object contains another. This is, again, valid for `jsonb` only:

```
SELECT * FROM product_info WHERE data @>
'{"product_category":"Stationary"}';
```

It will return all objects that contain the `product_category` key with the value stationary:

```
id |    data
---+----------------------------------------------------------------
 3 | {"product_name":"pen","product_category":"Stationary","price":"100"}
 4 | {"product_name":"pencil","product_category":"
Stationary","price":"50"}
 (2 rows)
```

The containment goes both ways:

```
SELECT * FROM product_info WHERE data <@
'{"product_category":"Stationary"}';
```

In this case, we will get the superset of the object. Since we don't have any record that has `{"product_category":"Stationary"}` as superset, we will get zero records:

```
id |    data
---+----------
 (0 rows)
```

Key/element existence

If we want to query the existence of a particular element, we can do it by ?. This is also only valid for `jsonb`:

```
SELECT * FROM product_info WHERE data ? 'Stationary';
id |    data
---+------------------------------------------------------------------
 3 | {"product_name":"pen","product_category":"Stationary","price":"100"}
 4 | {"product_name":"pencil","product_category":"
Stationary","price":"50"}
 (2 rows)
```

We can also test for objects that have any from a list of keys:

```
SELECT * FROM product_info WHERE data ?| array['pen', 'pencil'];
id |    data
---+------------------------------------------------------------------
 3 | {"product_name":"pen","product_category":"Stationary","price":"100"}
 4 | {"product_name":"pencil","product_category":"
Stationary","price":"50"}
```

Also you can test for the objects that have all the keys:

```
SELECT * FROM product_info WHERE data ?& array['pen', 'pencil'];
id |                  data
---+-----------------------------------------
 (0 rows)
```

We don't have any record that has both a pen and pencil.

Another way of querying JSON data is with the help of ->. The -> operator returns the original JSON type whereas ->> returns text:

```
SELECT id, data->'product_name' FROM product_info;
id  | data
----+----------
  1 | "chair"
  2 | "table"
  3 | "pen"
```

```
4 | "pencil"
```

You can select rows based on values from the JSON field:

```
SELECT product_name FROM product
WHERE data->>'product_category' = 'Stationary';
product_name
--------
pen
pencil
```

Outputting JSON

PostgreSQL also allows you to manipulate the existing tables and get the output in a JSON format.

Let's create a normal table and insert data into it:

```
CREATE TABLE product_info (id serial, product_name text, product_category
text, price int);
INSERT INTO product_info (product_name ,product_category , price)
VALUES ('Chair', 'Furniture', 200);
```

Now, since we have inserted the record in a normal way, we will change this to the JSON format. We will use the row_to_json function:

```
row_to_json
------------------------------------------------
{"f1":"Chair","f2":"Furniture","f3":200}
(1 row)
```

The field names have default values generated automatically by PostgreSQL. Similarly, we can output the array values as JSON with the help of the array_to_json function:

```
CREATE TABLE product_info(id serial, product_category text, product
text[]);
INSERT INTO product_info (product_category , product) VALUES
('Stationary', '{"Pen","Pencil"}');
```

Now, since the data has been inserted in the table, let's get this output as JSON:

```
SELECT row_to_json(row(product_category,array_to_json(product))) FROM
product_info;

row_to_json
-----------------------------------------
{"f1":"Stationary"," f2":['Pen','Pencil']}
```

```
(1 row)
```

Using XML in PostgreSQL

Like the JSON datatype, PostgreSQL provides `xml` datatypes as well, which helps us in storing XML data. The `xml` datatype is perhaps one of the more controversial types you'll find in a relational database. It comes with various functions to generate data, concatenate, and parse XML data, which we will discuss in further sections.

Inserting XML data in PostgreSQL

Like the JSON datatype, the `xml` datatype also make sure whether we are inserting the valid XML data or not. That is what makes the `xml` datatype different from a text datatype.

Let's create a table first and then we will insert data into it:

```
CREATE TABLE product_xml (id serial, info xml);
```

Now, since the `product_xml` table is created with a column having the `xml` datatype, let's insert some data in it:

```
INSERT INTO product_xml (info)
VALUES ('<product category>"Furniture">
<product_info><name> chair </name><price> 200</price></product_info>
<product_info><name> table </name><price> 500</price></product_info>
</product_category>');
```

We can always add a check constraint, making sure the price is always included with the product information using the `xpath_exists` function. This function basically evaluates the path of the XML string:

```
ALTER table product_xml add constraint check_price
CHECK(xpath_exists('/product_category/product_info/price',info));
```

Now, if you try to insert something like this:

```
INSERT INTO product_xml (info)
VALUES ('<product category ="Furniture"></product_category>');
```

It will error-out, telling us that it violates the `check_price` constraint. Similarly, there is the `xpath` function as well, which we will discuss in the next section.

Querying XML data

To query XML data, we can use the `xpath()` function. We will need to mention the path to get the required value. Let's consider querying the `product_xml` table, which we created in an earlier section:

```
SELECT xpath('/product_category/product_info/name/text()', product_info)
FROM product_xml;
Xpath
----------
Chair
table
```

It returns the value of `product_ name`.

Composite datatype

PostgreSQL supports a special datatype called composite datatype. The composite type represents the structure of a record or a row, which means it will have a list of fields and their datatypes. PostgreSQL supports using composite types in multiple ways, similar to how simple types can be used. A column of a table can be declared to be of a composite type.

Creating composite types in PostgreSQL

We can create or declare a composite datatype using the following syntax:

```
CREATE TYPE composite_type_name  AS (
Column_name1    any_datatype,
Column_name2    any_datatype
..
);
```

- `CREATE TYPE composite_type_name AS`: With this, PostgreSQL will help us create a composite datatype. The `composite_type_name` is the name of the composite type you want to define.
- `Column_name1 any_datatype`: You can provide the column that you want to declare accompanied by the datatype that you want to assign to the column.

The syntax of `CREATE TYPE` is similar to `CREATE TABLE`, except that you can only specify the field names and types; constraints, such as NOT NULL, cannot be included as part of this.

Let's try to create a composite datatype of a product with further details:

```
CREATE TYPE product AS (
Product_name text,
price numeric,
Product_category text
);
```

In the preceding example, we created a type with a name product with Product_name, price, and Product_category columns .

Now, since we discussed how we can declare a composite datatype, let's see how to use this composite type while creating a table:

```
CREATE TABLE supplier(
Supplier_name text,
Product_info   product
);
```

In the preceding example, we created the supplier table with a Supplier_name and a Product_info column. The Product_info column is of product datatype, which will automatically inherit its structure, including the column's product name, price, and product category.

There are two ways to insert data in composite columns. They are as follows:

- You can insert it as a literal constant—the field values need to be enclosed within parentheses and separated by commas. You can use double quotes around any field value, and must do so if it contains commas or parentheses. An example is shown, as follows:

  ```
  INSERT INTO supplier VALUES ('Supplier1',
  '("Table", 1000,"Furniture")');
  ```

- You can also use the ROW keyword while inserting the values in composite columns, but the ROW keyword is actually optional, except you have more than one field in the expression. In this case, you will need to use single quotes for the text field, as in the following example:

  ```
  INSERT INTO supplier VALUES ('Supplier2',
  ROW('Chair', 500,'Furniture'));
  ```

We need to use the ROW keyword while inserting the field values in composite datatype columns, like we did in the previous example to insert data for the product datatype.

So far, we have seen how we can declare composite datatype columns and insert the data. Now, let's discuss how to access a field of a composite column. You can use a dot followed by the field name, the way you do while selecting a field from a table name. For example, to select some subfields from our supplier table, we can use the following query:

```
SELECT (product_info).product_name
FROM supplier
WHERE (product_info).price > 500;
```

You can also use the table name, in which you have multiple tables, as shown in the following query:

```
SELECT (supplier.product_info).product_name
FROM supplier
WHERE (supplier.product_info).price > 500;

Product_name
--------------
Table
```

Altering composite types in PostgreSQL

To alter the definition of an existing composite type, we can use the ALTER TYPE keyword. There can be many things that we want to alter in a composite type, such as adding or removing a column. In this section, we will discuss similar scenarios.

To add a column in an existing composite type, we can use the following syntax:

```
ALTER TYPE type_name ADD ATTRIBUTE attribute_namedata_type[ COLLATE
collation ] [ CASCADE | RESTRICT ]
```

- ALTER TYPE: This changes the definition of an existing type.
- ADD ATTRIBUTE: This adds a new attribute to a composite type.
- CASCADE: This automatically applies the change to the table that we are using, the type which is being altered, and its successors.
- RESTRICT: This refuses the operation if the type is used by a typed table. This is the default.

Now, let's add a column in product type:

```
ALTER TYPE product ADD ATTRIBUTE unit_of_measureint CASCADE;
```

Similarly, to remove a column from ALTER TYPE type_name DROP ATTRIBUTE [IF EXISTS] attribute_name [CASCADE | RESTRICT]:

- DROP ATTRIBUTE [IF EXISTS]: This form drops an attribute from a composite type. If IF EXISTS is specified and the attribute does not exist, no error is thrown.

  ```
  ALTER TYPE product DROP ATTRIBUTE unit_of_measureint CASCADE;
  ```

  The same syntax will be used to alter the value of an attribute:

  ```
  ALTER TYPE type_name ALTER ATTRIBUTE attribute_name
  [ SET DATA ] TYPE
  data_type [ COLLATE collation ] [ CASCADE | RESTRICT ]
  ```

- SET DATA TYPE: This form changes the datatype of the attribute.

Dropping composite types in PostgreSQL

You can drop a composite type with the help of DROP TYPE. Simply using DROP TYPE will not drop any dependent tables, so you will have to use CASCADE like below:

```
DROP TYPE product CASCADE;
```

Summary

In this chapter, we looked at ways in which we can use the functionality of PostgreSQL using arrays, slicing arrays, and unnesting arrays of rows. An array provides great functionality when it comes to using data in multiple ways, or when we have a large chunk of data available with us. We also looked at the JSON datatype, which is useful to store multilevel, dynamically structured object graphs. Additionally, we discussed how to manage XML data and use its functions, which is supported by PostgreSQL. In the last section, we looked at ways to deal with composite types and altering types. Composite types are pretty important as once created they can be referred to by multiple tables, which helps in avoiding the same set of attributes again and again. Also, if we need to alter something in the set of those attributes, we will need to do it once and it will be automatically reflected in the dependent tables.

3
Triggers

In the previous chapter, we talked about a few data manipulation concepts of PostgreSQL; different complex data types, such as array, JSON, and XML; and how to handle them. In this chapter, we will discuss the basics, which will help you understand how triggers work in PostgreSQL and how to manage the PostgreSQL trigger, including modifying, disabling, and removing the trigger. Additionally, we will discuss trigger functions as well.

Introduction to triggers

A trigger is a specification that the database should run automatically whenever a certain type of operation is performed. It can be defined to run or fire either before or after any `INSERT`, `UPDATE`, or `DELETE` operation is performed on a particular object. This operation can be associated with a table, a view, a schema, or the database, and it is one of the following:

- A **Data Manipulation Language** (**DML**) statement—`DELETE`, `INSERT`, or `UPDATE`
- A **Data Definition Language** (**DDL**) statement—`CREATE`, `ALTER`, or `DROP`
- A database operation—`SERVERERROR`, `LOGON`, `LOGOFF`, `STARTUP`, or `SHUTDOWN`

Like a stored procedure, a trigger can be invoked repeatedly. A procedure is explicitly run by a user or an application but triggers are implicitly fired when a triggering event occurs, no matter which user is connected or which application is used. It can be enabled and disabled but you cannot explicitly invoke it. While a trigger is enabled, the database automatically invokes it—that is, the trigger fires—whenever its triggering event occurs. While a trigger is disabled, it does not get fired.

There are two type of triggers based on the level they are triggered at:

- **Row-level trigger**: An event is triggered for each row updated, inserted, or deleted
- **Statement-level trigger**: When a SQL statement emits an event, any triggers that are registered to listen for that event will be fired

Adding triggers to PostgreSQL

You can create a trigger with the CREATE TRIGGER statement. You are required to specify the triggering event in terms of triggering statements and the item on which they get fired. By default, a trigger is created in the enabled state.

The basic CREATE TRIGGER syntax is as follows:

```
CREATE [OR REPLACE ] TRIGGER trigger_name
{BEFORE | AFTER | INSTEAD OF} {event [OR ...]}
ON table_name
[FOR [EACH] {ROW | STATEMENT}]
EXECUTE PROCEDURE trigger_function;
```

Let's discuss the parameters of the preceding code syntax:

- CREATE [OR REPLACE] TRIGGER trigger_name: This creates a trigger with the given name or overwrites an existing trigger with the same name.
- BEFORE | AFTER | INSTEAD OF: This indicates the time when the trigger should get fired, for example, before or after updating a table. INSTEAD OF is used to create a trigger on a view. BEFORE and AFTER cannot be used to create a trigger on a view.
- {INSERT [OR] | UPDATE [OR] | DELETE}: This determines what operation a trigger should get fired at. The OR keyword can be utilized to use more than one triggering event. The trigger gets fired at all the specified triggering events.
- [ON table_name]: This identifies the name of the table or view with which the trigger is associated.
- [FOR EACH ROW]: This is used to determine whether a trigger must fire when each row gets affected (a row-level trigger) or just once when the entire SQL statement is executed (a statement-level trigger).
- WHEN (condition): This is valid only for row-level triggers. It is fired only for rows that satisfy the condition specified.

Let's create a trigger that helps in maintaining the history of employee salaries.

We can create a trigger to update the `emp_salary_history` table when an employee's salary is updated in the `employee` table.

First, we will create the `employee` table and the `emp_salary_history` table:

```
CREATE TABLE employee
(emp_id int4,
employee_name varchar(25),
department_id int4,
salary numeric(7,2));

CREATE TABLE emp_salary_history
emp_id int,,
employee_name varchar(25),
salary numeric(7,2)
Changed_on timestamp(6));
```

First, we will define a new function called `insert_into_salary_history`:

```
CREATE OR REPLACE FUNCTION insert_into_salary_history()
RETURNS trigger AS
$BODY$
BEGIN
INSERT INTO emp_salary_history VALUES
(:old.emp_id,
 :old.employee_name,
 :old.salary,
 Now());
END;
$BODY$
```

Let's create `emp_history_trigger` and execute it. This trigger will help you in inserting values in the employee history table before updating the `employee` table.

```
CREATE or REPLACE TRIGGER emp_history_trigger
BEFORE UPDATE OF salary
ON employee
FOR EACH ROW
EXECUTE PROCEDURE insert_into_salary_history();
```

Lets insert the data in the `employee` table:

```
INSERT INTO employee (emp_id,employee_name,department_id,salary)
VALUES (1, 'John',100,25000);
INSERT INTO employee (emp_id,employee_name,department_id,salary)
VALUES (2, 'Doe',110,30000);
```

And this is what the data will look like in the table:

```
SELECT * FROM employee;
```

emp_id	employee_name	department_id	Salary
1	John	100	25000
2	Doe	110	30000

Now, let's update the salary of an employee:

```
UPDATE EMPLOYEE SET salary = 26000 WHERE emp_id = 100
```

Let's see how the data looks after the update:

```
SELECT * FROM employee;
```

emp_id	employee_name	department_id	Salary
1	John	100	26000
2	Doe	110	30000

Once the preceding update query is executed, the trigger gets fired and it inserts data in the `emp_salary_history` table.

To view the records run the following query:

```
SELECT * FROM emp_salary_history;
```

emp_id	employee_name	Salary	Changed_on
1	John	25000	2015-05-12 15:21:00

If you ROLLBACK the transaction before committing to the database, the data inserted into the table is also rolled back.

Let's take another example. We discussed the different types of trigger earlier—row-level triggers and statement-level triggers. Through this example, we will see how it works.

This is the hierarchy followed when a trigger is fired. The BEFORE statement's trigger fires first. Next, the BEFORE row-level trigger fires, once for each row affected. Then the AFTER row-level trigger fires, once for each affected row. These events will alternate between the BEFORE and AFTER row-level triggers. Finally, the AFTER statement-level trigger fires.

Let's create a table, `emp_msg`, which we can use to store messages when triggers are fired:

```
CREATE TABLE emp_msg
(Message varchar(40),
 CurrentDate timestamp(15)
);
```

Let's create a BEFORE and AFTER statement and row-level triggers for the `employee` table:

- BEFORE UPDATE, statement level: This trigger will insert a record into the `emp_msg` table before a SQL update statement is executed at the statement level

  ```
  CREATE OR REPLACE FUNCTION Before_Update_Stat_employee_fnc()
  RETURNS trigger AS
  $BODY$
  BEGIN
  INSERT INTO emp_msg Values('Before update, statement level',now());
  END;
  $BODY$

  CREATE or REPLACE TRIGGER Before_Update_Stat_employee
  BEFORE UPDATE ON employee
  FOR EACH ROW
  EXECUTE PROCEDURE Before_Update_Stat_employee_fnc();
  ```

- BEFORE UPDATE, row level: This trigger will insert a record into the `emp_msg` table before each row is updated

  ```
  CREATE OR REPLACE FUNCTION Before_Update_Row_employee_fnc()
  RETURNS trigger AS
  $BODY$
  BEGIN
  INSERT INTO emp_msg Values('Before update, row level',now());
  END;
  $BODY$

  CREATE or REPLACE TRIGGER Before_Update_Row_employee()
  BEFORE UPDATE ON employee
  FOR EACH ROW
  EXECUTE PROCEDURE Before_Update_Row_employee_fnc();
  ```

- AFTER UPDATE, statement level: This trigger will insert a record into the `emp_msg` table after a SQL update statement is executed at the statement level

  ```
  CREATE OR REPLACE FUNCTION After_Update_Stat_employee_fnc()
  RETURNS trigger AS
  $BODY$
  ```

```
BEGIN
INSERT INTO emp_msg Values('After update, row level',now());
END;
$BODY$

CREATE or REPLACE TRIGGER After_Update_Stat_employee()
BEFORE UPDATE ON employee
FOR EACH ROW
EXECUTE PROCEDURE After_Update_Stat_employee_fnc();
```

- AFTER UPDATE, row level: This trigger will insert a record into the emp_msg table after each row is updated

```
CREATE OR REPLACE FUNCTION After_Update_Row_employee_fnc()
RETURNS trigger AS
$BODY$
BEGIN
INSERT INTO emp_msg Values('After update, row level',now());
END;
$BODY$

CREATE or REPLACE TRIGGER After_Update_Row_employee()
BEFORE UPDATE ON employee
FOR EACH ROW
EXECUTE PROCEDURE After_Update_Row_employee_fnc();
```

Now, let's execute an update statement on the table product:

```
UPDATE employee SET salary = 20000
WHERE emp_id IN (100,101);
```

Let's check the data in the emp_msg table to see the order in which the trigger is fired:

```
SELECT * FROM emp_msg order by current_date;
Output:
Mesage                            Current_Date
--------------------------------------------------------------
Before update, statement level    12-May-2015
Before update, row level          12-May-2015
After update, Row level           12-May-2015
Before update, row level          12-May-2015
After update, Row level           12-May-2015
After update, statement level     12-May-2015
```

The preceding result shows that the before update and after update row-level events have occurred twice as two records were updated. But the before update and after update statement-level events are fired only once for each SQL statement.

The preceding rules apply similarly to the INSERT and DELETE statements.

Modifying triggers in PostgreSQL

In order to modify the existing trigger, you can use the ALTER TRIGGER statement. The RENAME clause changes the name of the given trigger without otherwise changing the trigger definition. The syntax of the ALTER TRIGGER statement is as follows:

```
ALTER TRIGGER trigger_name ON table_name
RENAME TO new_name;
```

- ALTER TRIGGER: This statement helps you in modifying the existing trigger
- trigger_name: This is the name of an existing trigger to alter
- Table_name: This is the name of the table on which this trigger gets fired
- New_name: This is the new name for the trigger

Let's consider an example where you want to change the name of the emp_history_trigger trigger , which is associated with the employee table, to employee_salary_history_trigger. You can use the ALTER TRIGGER as follows:

```
ALTER TRIGGER  emp_history_trigger ON employee
RENAME TO employee_salary_history_trigger;
```

You can also disable an existing trigger using the ALTER TRIGGER command. The following is the syntax to disable the trigger with the ALTER statement:

```
ALTER TABLE table_name
DISABLE TRIGGER trigger_name | ALL
```

- ALTER TABLE table_name: This clause will alter the table on which the trigger is based.
- DISABLE TRIGGER trigger_name | ALL: This clause will disable the given trigger. If you want to disable all the triggers, then you don't need to mention the trigger name, and you can use the ALL keyword.

A disabled trigger will still exist in the database. It will not get fired when its triggering event occurs.

If you want to disable the `employee_salary_history_trigger` associated with the `employee` table, you can use the following statement:

```
ALTER TABLE employee
DISABLE TRIGGER employee_salary_history_trigger;
```

Removing a trigger function

To remove an existing trigger definition, you can use the DROP TRIGGER statement, as follows:

```
DROP TRIGGER [ IF EXISTS ] name ON table_name [ CASCADE | RESTRICT ]
```

- `IF EXISTS`: This will not throw an error if the trigger does not exist.
- `name`: This is the name of the trigger that has to be to removed.
- `table_name`: This is the name, optionally schema-qualified, of the table for which the trigger is defined.
- `CASCADE`: This automatically drops the objects that depend on the trigger.
- `RESTRICT`: This refuses to drop the trigger if any objects depend on it. This is the default. You can specify the trigger name that you want to remove after the DROP TRIGGER clause and the table with which the trigger is associated.

For example, to remove the `employee_salary_history_trigger` trigger, you can use the following statement:

```
DROP TRIGGER employee_salary_history_trigger ON employee CASCADE;
```

The preceding code line will drop all the objects that are dependent on `employee_salary_history_trigger`.

```
DROP TRIGGER employee_salary_history_trigger ON employee RESTRICT;
```

The preceding code line is by default and will not drop the trigger if any objects depend on it.

Creating a trigger function

PL/pgSQL allows us to make a trigger function. This trigger function is similar to an ordinary function but it does not have any parameter and has a return type trigger. A trigger fires when a condition is met and executes a special type of stored procedure called a trigger function.

PostgreSQL will call a trigger function when changes are being made to a particular table. The function must either return NULL or a row that matches the structure of the table for which the trigger function has been called.

As mentioned earlier, the trigger function is created as an ordinary function. The following is the syntax to create this:

```
CREATE FUNCTION trigger_function() RETURN trigger AS
```

The trigger function receives data about their calling environment through a special structure called **TriggerData**, which contains a set of local variables. For example, OLD and NEW represent the states of a row in the table before or after the triggering event. PostgreSQL provides other local variables with TG_ as the prefix, such as TG_WHEN, TG_TABLE_NAME, and so on. Let's discuss these procedure variables in more detail.

The PostgreSQL trigger procedure variables are as follows:

- NEW: This is a record containing the new database row
- OLD: This is a record containing the old database row
- TG_NAME: This is a variable containing the name of the trigger that fired and caused the trigger procedure to run
- TG_WHEN: This is a text variable containing the text before or after, depending on the type of the trigger
- TG_LEVEL: This is a text variable containing the row or statement, depending on the trigger definition
- TG_OP: This is a text variable containing INSERT, DELETE, or UPDATE, depending on the event that occurred resulting in this trigger being fired
- TG_RELID: This is an object identifier representing the table the trigger is activated on
- TG_RELNAME: This is the name of the table that the trigger has been fired on
- TG_NARGS: This is an integer variable containing the number of arguments specified in the trigger definition
- TG_ARGV: This is an array of strings containing the procedure parameters starting at zero; the invalid indexes return NULL values

Testing the trigger function

Let's create a trigger function to capture the history transferred from multiple departments.

We have an employee table with the following structure:

```
CREATE TABLE employee(
  Emp_id int4,
  emp_name varchar(40),
  dept_id int4,
  salary numeric(7,2));
```

We also have an employee_dept_history table with the following structure:

```
CREATE TABLE employee_dept_history(
  Emp_id int4,
  emp_name varchar(40),
  dept_id int4,
  date_changed_on  timestamp(6));
```

Now, let's create the trigger function:

```
CREATE OR REPLACE FUNCTION emp_dept_changes()
RETURNS trigger AS
$BODY$
BEGIN
IF NEW.dept_id <> OLD.dept_id THEN
INSERT INTO employee_dept_history (emp_id,emp_name,dept_id,date_changed_on)
VALUES(OLD.id,OLD.emp_name,OLD.dept_id,now());
END IF;
RETURN NEW;
END;
$BODY$ LANGUAGE 'plpgsql';
```

The function checks whether the department ID of the employee changes. It will insert the old department ID into the employee_dept_history table, including the employee ID, department ID, and the date of change.

Additionally, within this trigger function, two very special records are made available: OLD and NEW. These records contain (for row triggers) the data from the row being affected by the UPDATE that fired the trigger. The OLD contains data from before the UPDATE, and NEW contains data from after the update (or the proposed UPDATE for a BEFORE trigger).

Now, we will create the trigger that will use the trigger function. Before the department ID column is updated, the trigger function is automatically invoked to log the change.

```
CREATE TRIGGER  emp_dept__changes_trg
  BEFORE UPDATE
  ON employee
  FOR EACH ROW
  EXECUTE PROCEDURE emp_dept_changes ();
```

We can insert some sample data to test. We will insert two records into the `employee` table, as shown in the following code snippet:

```
INSERT INTO employee (emp_id, emp_name, dept_id, salary)
VALUES ('1', 'John','100','25000');

INSERT INTO employee (emp_id, emp_name, dept_id, salary)
VALUES ('2', 'Doe','101','30000');
```

The `employee` table has two records now.

Let's update the department ID of `emp_id = 1`:

```
UPDATE employee
SET dept_id= '102'
WHERE emp_id = 1;
```

The trigger function is called whenever an UPDATE takes place on the `employee` table. When we run the update query, before updating the record, the `emp_dept__changes_trg` trigger will get fired, which in turn will call the trigger function, `emp_dept_changes`. The trigger function will check if the old department ID, which is 100, matches the new department ID, which is 102. As they are not equal, it will insert the data in the `employee_dept_history` table.

Viewing existing triggers

In order to view all the triggers that exist in the database, you can query the PG_TRIGGER table. This stores information about the header and body of the trigger.

```
SELECT * FROM pg_trigger
WHERE tgname = 'employee_salary_history_trigger';
```

The preceding query provides the header and body of the `employee_salary_history_trigger` trigger.

Summary

In this chapter, we looked at ways in which we can extend the functionality of PostgreSQL queries through triggers. You learned that PostgreSQL triggers can use trigger functions, which enhance the functionality of triggers. As discussed in this chapter, triggers can be used as an alternative method to implement referential integrity constraints. By using triggers, business rules and transactions are easy to store in the database and can be used consistently even if there are future updates to the database. When a change happens in a database, a trigger can adjust the change to the entire database using the INSERT, UPDATE, or DELETE statements. In the next chapter, we will talk about some important aspects of database design, what makes a good database, and database design practices.

4
Understanding Database Design Concepts

When it comes to designing a database, it is very important that we understand database design concepts first. Having less understanding or having some doubts, can lead to a bad database design, which can give rise to a number of problems for users, some of which are as follows:

- Inability to fulfill report requirement
- Loss of data integrity over time
- Redundancy
- Bad performance
- Primary key on multiple fields

Basic design rules

There are some basic design rules which help us to build a good database. Let us discuss on those:

The ability to solve the problem

The main reason for designing a database is to solve a problem. So, it's very important to understand the problem and build the database so that it can fulfill the business requirements. No matter how well a database is designed, it is worthless if it doesn't solve the reporting requirements.

The ability to hold the required data

The main reason for having a database is to store data. While thinking about this concept, you should first consider what is required in order to fulfill the needed queries, the must have fields and after that, you can go ahead and extend the design so that it can fulfill any future requirements.

The ability to support relationships

Relationships are equally as important as defining the entities. A database should support relationships among the entities. If you don't focus on the relationships, your database design will end up excessively complex and might suffer from data integrity issues.

The ability to impose data integrity

Data integrity plays a very vital role in a database. The entire purpose of the database is to store correct and high-quality data so that it can provide useful information when needed. Many real-time databases may have deficiencies because of handwritten forms that have missing information. This is just one example of data integrity that may cause further deterioration in the quality of the data.

The ability to impose data efficiency

In a largely built database, there are cases where performance may not be up to the desired expectations. And, achieving more practical goals may spoil the purity of the design. The steps for the optimized design should be considered with the utmost priority before you even consider any optimization. A properly indexed database may drastically improve the performance of the database. Another simple method can be to rewrite queries, which can provide dramatic performance improvements without hampering the core design. Things that you can avoid to maintain the database is changing a varchar to the char type or experimenting with indexes on different attributes. This is just a waste of time and resources that will result in a poor performance and inconsistent database schema, which is difficult to maintain. The first and foremost step is to check and provide the solution in the application design if there are any bottlenecks. Redesigning the database should be the last resort when it comes to an optimized system. With this consideration, a quote stated from Donald Knuth (Professor Emeritus of *The Art of Computer Programming* at Stanford University), *"Premature optimization is the root of all evil"*, should make more sense now.

The ability to accommodate future changes

In the software industry, people are generally surprised at just how long software remains in use, even well beyond the design's lifetime. And when it comes to databases, this becomes even more noticeable. The reason for this is that, migrating the data from an old legacy system to the new one is often a significant problem in its own right. There is always a constant pressure to enhance the existing database design rather than start from scratch and then migrate the data at a later stage. It's often noticeable that any change that you make to your database to improve the efficiency makes your design harder to evolve.

Normalization

No database design is complete without discussing database anomalies, normal forms, and database normalization. As we have gone through the various design stages, we can now see how the final design will be formed based on these rules. The origin of database normalization was revealed by E.F. Codd in 1969, published in *Communications of the ACM, Vol. 13, No. 6, June 1970*.

In this work, normal forms were defined and each normal form was built on a previous rule and applies more stringent requirements to the design. In a religious normalization theory, there are five normal forms, for example, the Boyce-Codd normal form. But in reality, you will be amazed to know that only the first three forms are commonly used, and we will discuss them in the detail in this chapter.

A normalized database is easy to maintain and manage. All of this can be achieved using the first three normal forms. Databases that are designed without keeping in mind normalization will always have performance issues and are more inclined to store invalid data.

Anomalies in DBMS

Broadly, we have three types of anomalies that will occur when the database is not normalized. These are the insertion, update, and deletion anomalies. Let's consider each one of them with an example.

For example, suppose a company stores employee details in a table named `employee` that has four attributes: `emp_id` to store the employee's id, `emp_name` to store the employee's name, `emp_address` to store the employee's address, and `emp_dept` to store the department details (where the employee works). At the initial stage, the table will look like this:

emp_id	emp_name	emp_address	emp_dept
101	Roger	Texas	D001
101	Roger	Texas	D002
123	Martin	Ohio	D890
166	George	New York	D900
166	George	New York	D004

As you can see, the preceding table is not normalized. We will start to see the following problems when a table is not normalized:

- **Update anomaly:** In the preceding table, we have two rows for employee `George` as he belongs to two departments of the company. If we want to update the address of `George`, then we have to update it in two rows or the data will become inconsistent. If, somehow, the correct address gets updated in one department but not in the other, then, as per the database, `George` will have two different addresses, which is not correct and will lead to inconsistent data.
- **Insert anomaly:** Suppose a new employee joins the company, and is under training and currently not assigned to any department, then we will not be able to insert the data into the table if the `emp_dept` field doesn't allow nulls.
- **Delete anomaly:** Suppose, the company closes the department `D890`, then deleting the rows that have `emp_dept` as `D890` will also delete all the information for employee `Martin`, as he is assigned only to this department.

To overcome these anomalies, we will need to normalize the data. In the next section, we will discuss normalization.

First normal form

In linewith the rule of **first normal form** (**1NF**), an attribute (column) of a table cannot hold multiple values. It should hold only atomic values and it cannot be further subdivided into repeating groups. For example, in our database design, we divided the vendor name into a title, first name, and last name. There may arise a situation where we will have to use them separately. So, storing them as individual attributes will allow us to achieve this.

Having no repeating groups suggests that the data should be consistent and the groups for any employee should not be repeated. A simple example to explain this will be using a simple worksheet to store vendors and their orders. Once a vendor has more than one order, we have repeating information for that vendor, and our worksheet will no longer have the same number of rows in all columns.

If we store both the first and last name in the `fname` column of our `Vendor` table, then this will go against the 1NF because the column `fname` will actually be holding both the names. We will need to store the names separately so that consistency can be maintained.

Second normal form

A table is said to be in the **second normal form** (**2NF**) if:

- It is in 1NF
- No nonprime attribute is dependent on the proper subset of any candidate key of the table

In other words, it means that no information in a row depends on only a part of the primary key. For example, in our `ORDERINFO` table, we stored the date that the order was placed in this table, as shown in the following table:

Column name	Datatype
ORDER_ID	INTEGER
ITEM_ID	INTEGER
NO_OF_QUANTITY	INTEGER
DATE_ORDER_PLACED	DATE

In the preceding table, (ORDERINFO), we can see that the breaking 2NF will recall that our primary key for ORDERINFO is a candidate key of ORDER_ID and ITEM_ID. The date on which the order was placed depends on only the ORDER_ID column, and not on the item ordered. Therefore, this will have violated 2NF.

In some scenarios, you may encounter that you are storing data that looks as if it might go against the 2NF but, in reality, it does not. For instance, if we change our prices frequently, customers will rightly expect to pay the price shown on the day they ordered and not on the day it was shipped.

In order to accomplish this, we will need to store the selling price in the ORDERINFO table to record the price on the date on which the order was placed. This will not violate 2NF, because the price stored in the ORDERINFO table will depend on both the item and the actual order.

Third normal form

A table is said to be in **third normal form** (**3NF**) if both the following conditions are true:

- The table must be in 2NF
- Transitive functional dependency of nonprime attribute on any super key should be removed

An attribute that is not part of any candidate key is known as a nonprime attribute. This form is very closely tied to the 2NF but is more general. It says that no information in an attribute that is not the primary key can depend on anything except the primary key.

Suppose, in the Vendor table, we stored a vendor's age and DOB as shown in the following table. This will violate 3NF because the vendor's age depends on the DOB, a non-key column, as well as the actual customer, which is given by VENDOR_ID (primary key).

Column name	Datatype
VENDOR_ID	INTEGER
TITLE	VARCHAR (4)
FIRST NAME	VARCHAR (100)
LAST NAME	VARCHAR (100)
ADDRESS	VARCHAR (100)
POSTAL CODE	VARCHAR (100)

COUNTY	VARCHAR (100)
COUNTRY	VARCHAR (100)
DOB	DATE

Although the preferred solution is to make your database reach to the 3NF, there are situations when it's necessary to break the rules. This process is called denormalizing the database. You should always consider designing the database in a fully normalized way. However, you can denormalize it when you have a major problem with performance.

Common patterns

There are many situations that will occur repeatedly when you design or build a database. We normally call them common patterns. It is very important that you understand these patterns as they are solved in the same way, or the strategy to solve them will be similar, and that will save your time. Here, we will discuss some common problems and patterns and how we can solve or implement them.

Many-to-many relationships

Before we discuss how to implement a many-to-many relationship, let's discuss what exactly this many-to-many relationship is.

If a row in a table is associated with one or more rows in other table and a row in other table is associated with one or more rows in first table, then it's called many-to-many relationship. An example of a many-to-many relationship is a table of orders and products. Now, one order might have one or more products and a product can be ordered by one or more orders.

It is never recommended you implement a many-to-many relationship in a database, so you will need to insert a table that will have a one-to-many relationship with both the main tables. We call it the Link table. Now, this particular table will have a primary key from both the tables. So, the primary key of the first table or the primary key of the second table may occur multiple times but the combination of both primary keys, which we can use as the surrogate key, will exist only once.

Let's consider the preceding example using `Orders` and `Products`. In order to implement a many-to-many relationship between two, take the third table, as order details.

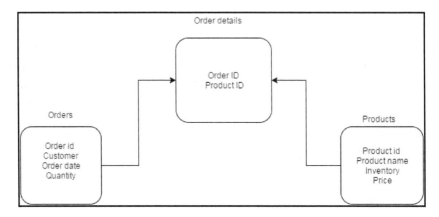

Now `Order id` is the primary key of the `Orders` table and `Product id` is the primary key of the `Products` table. Both are foreign keys in the `Order details` table. But, together, they form a surrogate key in the `Order details` table and will form a primary key there, which means that the combination of `Order id` and `Product id` will be unique.

Hierarchy

Another pattern is a hierarchy. Now, a hierarchy is basically a parent-child relationship. Suppose we have a product inventory that is located in a state and country; you can implement the following model, which is not ideal:

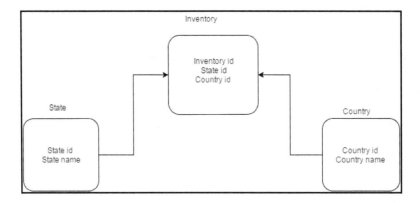

The problem with this model is that, while inserting the `Country id`, there is no constraint that will check whether the state comes under what `Country`, which doesn't complete the hierarchy as such.

In order to make sure that a parent-child relationship is followed, we can implement the following model, which makes sure that the hierarchy is maintained, and also a direct relationship between `State` and `Country`.

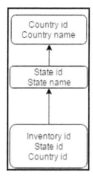

Recursive relationships

This is another pattern commonly encountered while building a database. So far, we have talked about the relationships between two entities or tables. But, there can also be a scenario where an entity has a relationship with itself, which we call a recursive relationship.

Let's consider a basic example of `Employee` and `Supervisor`. In every department, an employee is supervised by a supervisor and of course, all the employees are not supervisors. So, in order to visualize this example, refer to the following diagram:

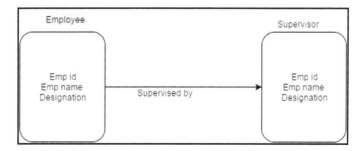

Although, for visualization, the preceding diagram is okay, this is not the correct way to achieve it in a database. The problem with this model is that each manager is also an employee. If we build the `Supervisor` table, we will have duplicate information in both tables, which will lead to redundancy.

In order to implement a recursive relationship in a database, it is better to add another column as `supervisor_id` to record which employee is supervised by whom and relate it to the same table.

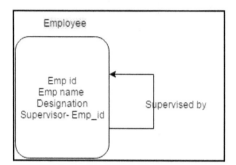

Now, the `Supervisor` field will have an employee ID for the supervisor. In order to query employees and their supervisors, we will join the `Employee` table to itself using aliases.

```
SELECT e.emp_name AS "Employee name", m.emp_name AS "Manager name"
FROM Employee e LEFT OUTER JOIN Employee M
ON E.supervisor_id = M.emp_iD
```

We have an outer join here in order to make sure that the employees also comes in the result that is not supervised by anyone.

Summary

In this chapter, we talked about what problems you will face if your database is not designed properly and how to overcome them. It gives you a good idea of what we should keep in mind while designing a database. Additionally, we also discussed database anomalies, normal forms, and database normalization. In the next chapter, we will talk about transactions and locking. We will cover how to start and manage a transaction using different kinds of isolation level. We will explain each kind of transaction level with examples. We will also cover the locking mechanism available in PostgreSQL and how we can best use it to benefit from locking.

5
Transactions and Locking

So far in this book, we have discussed basic and advanced concepts of PostgreSQL and a few database designing concepts. In this chapter, we will discuss multiuser aspects of PostgreSQL. In the real world, an application being accessed by multiple users at the same time is very generic and it becomes important that we understand these concepts. We will look at two important concepts of database support for multiple users: transactions and locking.

Transaction means a combination of different changes made to the database in a single unit. And when we talk about multiuser environment, which means that multiple users are trying to access the database at the same time, it's very important that multiple transactions are not impacting each other. So, we will discuss the challenges that we face in multiuser environments and different levels of isolation, which is required to control the concurrency. Additionally, we will discuss the different techniques of locking.

Defining transactions

In the previous chapters, we mentioned that we should try and write all the database changes with a single declarative statement. However, when it comes to reality, there comes a time when you cannot write everything to a database using one single SQL statement. This doesn't mean it will be just one single SQL statement; there might be multiple statements that will update the database correctly. If, by chance, any problem is encountered in the statement or a group of statements, then none of the database changes should be written. In other words, you will require the SQL statements to work as an individual unit and execute tasks sequentially in a way that allows the changes to be reversed and hides uncommitted changes from other processes. In this case, either all of the statements should be executing successfully or none of them should be executing.

A real-world example can be taken from the banking domain, where all transactions are recorded in debit and credit. So, we can consider the case of two accounts in the bank residing in different tables in the database so that, when one account is debited, the other should be credited. If, in any case, you debit one account and fail to credit the second account, you must return the money to the first account. In other words, you act as if nothing happened in the first place. No bank will remain in business if the money disappears when transferring between accounts.

For example, let's consider that we want to record a payment of $1,000 from John's account to Smith's account. Using SQL statements, the situation will look like this:

```
UPDATE accounts SET balance = balance - 1000
WHERE name = 'John';

UPDATE branches SET balance = balance - 1000
WHERE name = (SELECT branch_name FROM accounts WHERE name = 'John');

UPDATE accounts SET balance = balance + 1000
WHERE name = 'Smith';

UPDATE branches SET balance = balance + 1000
WHERE name = (SELECT branch_name FROM accounts WHERE name = 'Smith');
```

With the preceding statements, as you can see, there are several steps involved when doing simple debit and credit operations. The bank official will have to make sure that either all these updates happen or none of them happen. So, we will need to guarantee that if something goes wrong midway then none of the steps executed so far should take effect. We can achieve this guarantee if we group the update statements together. A transaction is said to be atomic from the point of view of other transactions; it either happens completely or not at all.

ACID rules

Atomicity, Consistency, Isolation, and Durability (ACID) is a frequently used acronym to describe the four properties a transaction must have:

- **Atomicity**: A transaction, no matter if it contains multiple actions on the database, should happen as a one-individual unit. It should happen only once, with no repetition of the actions. In our banking example, the money movement must be atomic. The debiting of one account and crediting of another must take place as one single action, no matter how many SQL statements are a part of that unit.

- **Consistency**: The point of consistency is that there is no point where the transaction is partially committed. In our banking example, all the accounts maintained by the bank should accurately reflect the correct debit and credit balances; otherwise, it will create a huge problem for the bank to determine the root cause.
- **Isolation**: This means that every transaction, irrespective of how many, is a part of that group and must behave as an independent transaction. A good example of this is of the ticketing system. If there is only one seat available in the online booking for a train, and two customers, both from different locations, are trying to buy it, then a system will be smart enough to isolate both the transactions, and the ticket will be booked to only one customer. This will require a multiuser database that can distinguish the transactions independently.
- **Durability**: This means that once the transaction is completed, it should remain completed in the database. Once the money transaction is done successfully, it should remain saved in the database even if the power fails or the machine running the database has an uncontrolled power down. In PostgreSQL, this can be achieved using transactional log files (Write-Ahead Log files). Transaction durability is a system feature and it can happen without the user intervention.

Effect of concurrency on transactions

Before we discuss the effect of concurrency on transactions, let's discuss what concurrency is. Concurrency allows multiple users to access, select, or update the data at the same time. This is a very simple scenario where more than one user is trying to query the same. As users are just executing the SELECT statement, the database will give data to both the users. But, what if one user is trying to update the data and the other is trying to query the same data? In such cases, concurrency is a big problem.

When the transactions are being made concurrently, the following are the challenges that occur:

- Concurrent transactions are executed with the proper behavior, which means serializability is maintained. The transactions should be isolated and have no effect on each other.
- Most of the concurrent transactions face performance issues. Though we execute one transaction at a time, it will impact the performance if high-volume data is there. In short, ACID consistency requirements lead to performance issues when transactions overlap. So, ideally, no transaction should block each other.

Transactions and savepoints

So far, we have discussed basic transactions along with their syntax. In this section, we will discuss savepoints, which are useful to roll back to a particular point in the transaction.

In other words, we can say that a savepoint is a mark in a transaction that will allow us to rollback all the commands executed after that, and it will restore the transaction state during the time of the savepoint. Once you have defined the savepoint in a transaction, you can use rollback to command to the savepoint whatever you have declared in the transaction.

The following is the syntax for this:

```
BEGIN
First SQL;
Second SQL;
SAVEPOINT test_savepoint;
Third SQL;
ROLLBACK TO test_savepoint;
Forth SQL;
COMMIT;
```

Let's take an example to illustrate the same:

```
BEGIN;
UPDATE product SET price = price+100
   WHERE product_name = 'Chair';
SAVEPOINT test_savepoint;
UPDATE product SET price = price+200
   WHERE product_name = 'Table';
ROLLBACK TO test_savepoint;
UPDATE product SET price = price+100
   WHERE product_name = 'Table';
COMMIT;
```

In the previous example, we updated the `price` of the `product` and increased it by `100`, then updated the `price` of the table by `200` and rolled back to the savepoint. After rolling back to the savepoint, it will still be defined so that you can roll back to it several times. However, if you are sure you won't need to roll back to a particular savepoint again, it can be released. Releasing a savepoint removes the released savepoint, and removes any saveopints defined between the released savepoint and the release command. Rolling back to a savepoint undoes all transactions defined between the savepoint and the rollback, including any savepoints in that region.

Transaction isolation

As discussed in the earlier section, transactions that need to work for multiple concurrent users must be isolated from each other. It is really difficult to manage this isolation when different users are performing updates on the same data. Although, we can impose a limit, that one single connection to the database makes sure that only a single transaction is being executed at any one time. However, in that case, multiuser performance will be impacted.

Implementing isolation levels

The SQL standard has defined different isolation levels on the basis of phenomena that are expected to occur in a multiuser database while transactions are interacting. These phenomena are called dirty reads, unrepeatable reads, and phantom reads. Let's discuss each of them and then we will discuss how isolation levels are defined.

Dirty reads

If one transaction is able to see the uncommitted work of another transaction, that will be an example of a dirty read.

As we discussed in the earlier section, a transaction is a group of multiple SQL statements and should be atomic, which means that either all components of a transaction get executed or none of them get executed. So, there could be a scenario where uncommitted work is visible to other transactions, however not yet committed or rolled back. Therefore, no other users of the database should see this changed data before a commit.

Let's take the following example to illustrate the difference between behavior when a dirty read is allowed versus when it is not allowed.

Transaction 1	Data seen by transaction 1	Data seen by other transactions with dirty reads allowed	Data seen by other transactions with dirty reads not allowed
BEGIN	200	200	200
UPDATE product SET price=500 where product_name='Chair'	500	500	200
COMMIT	500	500	500

BEGIN	500	500	500
UPDATE product SET price=700 where product_name='Chair'	700	700	500

Non-repeatable reads

If a transaction were able to read a row, and then later read the same row and see different values based on the work of another statement, that would be an unrepeatable read. It is very much similar to dirty reads. By default, PostgreSQL allows unrepeatable reads.

Let's consider the following example to understand this more clearly:

Transaction 1	Data seen by transaction 1	Data seen by other transactions with unrepeatable reads allowed	Data seen by other transactions with unrepeatable reads not allowed
BEGIN	200	200	200
UPDATE product SET price=500 where product_name='Chair'	500	200	200
COMMIT	500	500	200
			COMMIT
Select price from product where product_name='Chair'	500	500	500

In the preceding example, we see that if unrepeatable reads are allowed, other transactions will able to see the data committed by transaction 1 without getting committed. On the contrary, if unrepeatable reads are not allowed, the other transactions will not able to read the data committed by transaction 1 and will have to commit exclusively to read the latest value.

Phantom reads

If a transaction were able to read a set of rows matching some logical condition, and later read that same logical set of rows and see new ones, which qualify because of the work of another transaction, that would be a phantom read. A phantom read describes a set of data rows, while a dirty read refers to a specific value from the same row. A transaction always sees its own work. By default, PostgreSQL will allow phantom reads.

Let's take a look at the following example to get a better understanding on this:

Transaction 1	Transaction 2
BEGIN	BEGIN
UPDATE product SET price = price + 100;	
	INSERT INTO product(....) VALUES (...);
COMMIT;	
	COMMIT;

In the preceding example, transaction 1 is incrementing the price of the product by 100. Before this transaction is committed, transaction 2 inserts another row in the table.

Therefore, we might expect that the price of the new product will be incremented by 100.

If a phantom read occurs, however, the new record that appears after transaction 1 determines which rows to UPDATE, and the price of the new item does not get incremented.

ANSI isolation levels

The ANSI standard defines different isolation levels that are used by a database in combinations of the earlier discussed phenomena-dirty reads, unrepeatable reads, and phantom reads.

Transaction isolation levels

Below table explains the behavior of different types of reads against different isolation levels:

Isolation level	Dirty read	Non-repeatable read	Phantom read
Read Uncommitted	Possible	Possible	Possible
Read Committed	Not possible	Possible	Possible
Repeatable Read	Not possible	Not possible	Possible
Serializable	Not possible	Not possible	Not possible

As you saw in the preceding table, moving from the Read Uncommitted to Serializable level, the phenomena behavior is reducing.

Changing the isolation level

PostgreSQL defaults to the Read Committed isolation mode.

You can change the isolation level using the Set Transaction Isolation Level command.

The following is the syntax to change the isolation level:

```
SET TRANSACTION ISOLATION LEVEL { SERIALIZABLE | REPEATABLE READ | READ
COMMITTED | READ UNCOMMITTED }
```

The Set Transaction command will have an impact on the current transaction only. There will not be any impact on the other transactions.

This Set Transaction command has to be executed before you execute any DML (SELECT, INSERT, DELETE, UPDATE) statement. If you are executing it after the first query or DML statement, then changing the transaction-isolation level will not have any impact on the transaction. In other words, you will not be able to change the transaction level in this scenario.

Using explicit and implicit transactions

You must be wondering why, before this chapter, we carried out our transactions without using a `Begin` command, whereas throughout this chapter, we have used `BEGIN` and `COMMIT` or `ROLLBACK`, to complete our transactions. So, what is the advantage of using the `BEGIN` command if we can do our transactions without using it?

Whenever it comes to updating data, PostgreSQL, by default, works in implicit transaction mode, which means auto-commit mode. It is okay for new users but it is not recommended for real applications where we want to have explicit transactions with the `COMMIT` or `ROLLBACK` statements.

In other RDBMS systems, you will need to explicitly issue a command to switch to explicit mode, but with PostgreSQL, just by issuing the `BEGIN` command, will automatically switch to explicit mode until the `COMMIT` or `ROLLBACK` statements are issued.

Avoiding deadlocks

What if two different sessions are trying to run a DML statement on the same data at the same time? There will always be a risk of deadlock. The following is an example of deadlock:

Session 1	Session 2
`UPDATE emp SET ... WHERE id = 1`	
	`UPDATE emp SET ... WHERE id = 2`
`UPDATE emp SET ... WHERE id = 2`	
	`UPDATE emp SET ... WHERE id = 1`

In this example, both the sessions are blocked as both sessions are waiting on each other to release.

Session 1, transaction 1 locks the row with `id = 1` to update the record. Now, Session 2 transaction 1 does the same and acquires the row-level locks on the row with `id = 2`. Session 1 transaction 2 is trying to acquire the lock on the row with `id = 2`, but cannot, and record with `id = 2` is locked by session 2, so session 1 will wait for session 2 to release the lock. Coming to session 2, transaction 2 will try to acquire the lock on row with `id = 1` for the update, but since it is being locked by session 1, it will wait for session 1 to release the lock. Thus, both session waits on each other, which a deadlock condition.

In this scenario, PostgreSQL will detect the deadlock and cancel one of the transactions.

There is no certainty which session PostgreSQL will choose to cancel, but it will try to pick the one that it considers to have done the least work.

We should always develop our code in such a way that it should prevent deadlocks from occurring. One of the simplest techniques is to try and keep your transactions as short as possible. The fewer records and tables involved in a transaction, the less time the locks will be held and the less chance of deadlock. Another technique is to always process tables and records in the same order.

In the preceding example, if both sessions tried to update the rows in the same order, there would not be a deadlock scenario. Session 1 would be able to update both its rows and complete, while Session 2 would wait till session 1 is complete. Explicit locking might be another way to avoid the deadlock, which we will be covering in the next section.

Explicit locking

There may come a time when you realize that the automatic locking PostgresSQL provides is not sufficient for your needs.

In order to fulfill your needs, you can explicitly lock the rows or, perhaps, an entire table.

In line with the SQL standards you will never see an option that will allow you to lock a table. One should only use explicit locking in urgent scenarios.

Locks for rows or tables are only allowed inside the transaction. Once the transaction gets completed with a commit or rollback, all the locks acquired during the transaction will be released automatically.

An explicit lock cannot be released during the transaction because releasing the lock on a row that is being modified during a transaction might allow another application to change it. This in turn will not allow the rollback to the initial changes.

Locking rows

Deadlocks can be avoided if we can lock the number of rows prior to making changes to them. Locking rows prior to making the changes will allow you to restrict the changes that will be made by other applications—this will not allow the conflict part to happen.

To lock a set of rows, we can use a SELECT statement and append a FOR UPDATE, as shown in the following example:

```
SELECT 1 FROM items WHERE unit_price > 15.0 FOR UPDATE;
```

This will lock all the rows in the items where the unit_price is greater than 15.0. As we don't need any rows to be returned, we used 1 as a convenient way of minimizing the data returned.

Consider the scenario where we want to lock all the rows in the employees table where the employees live in Chicago because we need to change the telephone code, as the area code is being split into several new ones. We will need to make sure that we can access all the rows, but we will require some procedural code to then process each row in turn, calculating what the new telephone code should be.

```
=> BEGIN

BEGIN
bpfinal => SELECT customer_id FROM employees WHERE town = 'Chicago' FOR
UPDATE;

employee_id
-------------
4
8
(2 rows)
```

The two rows with employee_id values 4 and 8 are locked, and we can test this by trying to update them in a different psql session:

```
BEGIN
=> UPDATE customer SET phone = '555-4444' WHERE employee_id = 4;
UPDATE 1
=> UPDATE customer SET phone = '555-8888' WHERE employee_id = 8;
```

At this point, the second session gets blocked until we press *Ctrl + C* to interrupt it, or the first session commits or rolls back.

At the beginning, the SELECT ... FOR UPDATE returns the rows with employee_ id values 4 and 8 to be locked. Other sessions are able to update different rows in the employees table, but not rows 4 and 8 until the transaction is completed and the locks are released.

Locking tables

PostgreSQL provides the functionality to lock the full table, although we don't recommend using table lock if at all possible. You should comply with the other SQL standard mechanisms that ensure client isolation.

The syntax to lock tables is as follows:

```
LOCK [ TABLE ] table-name
LOCK [ TABLE ] table-name IN [ ROW | ACCESS ] { SHARE | EXCLUSIVE } MODE
LOCK [ TABLE ] table-name IN SHARE ROW EXCLUSIVE MODE
```

The simplest syntax that is used by the application generally is as follows:

```
LOCK TABLE table-name
```

This is the same as the following:

```
LOCK TABLE table-name ACCESS EXCLUSIVE MODE
```

This type of lock doesn't allow any application to access the table in any way. However, this type of a lock is rarely used unless it is required in certain circumstances.

Summary

In this chapter, we closely observed how transactions and locking work. We noticed how, in a single-user database, transactions are useful because they allow you to bind together SQL statements in a single atomic unit. We also covered the multiuser environment for the transactions. Then, we moved to the standard-isolation levels of ANSI SQL for their undesirable phenomena and how we can eliminate different types of undesirable behavior by defining various levels of transaction consistency. We also covered how we could end up with performance degradation by eliminating desirable features. Therefore, it becomes very essential to strike a balance between the ideal behavior and acceptable performance. We explored locking, and using simple techniques we can overcome the risk of deadlocks—a situation where two or more applications can freeze, waiting for the other to complete. We also did explicit locking, which provides the functionality to lock specific rows in a table or the entire table within a transaction.

However, transactions and locking do not directly modify data, which is what most database programmers really want to do. Understanding how these important features of SQL work is critical to being able to write applications that safely use and update data in a database.

In the next chapter, we will discuss indexes and constraints, which will allow you to understand performance improvement techniques in a more interesting way.

6
Indexes and Constraints

In the previous chapter, we talked about transactions and locking, which helped you understand their effect on the database. In this chapter, we will discuss indexes and constraints, types of indexes and constraints, their use in the real world, and the best practices on when we need to and how to create them. Your application may have different kinds of data, and you will want to maintain data integrity across the database and, at the same time, you need a performance gain as well. This chapter helps you understand how you can choose indexes and constraints for your requirement and improve performance. It also covers real-time examples that will help you understand better. Of course, not all types of indexes or constraints are the best fit for your requirement; however, you can choose the required ones based on how they work.

Introduction to indexes and constraints

An index is a pointer to the actual rows in its corresponding table. It is used to find and retrieve particular rows much faster than using the standard method. Indexes help you improve the performance of queries. However, indexes get updated on every **Data Manipulation Language** (**DML**)—that is, INSERT, UPDATE, and DELETE—query on the table, which is an overhead, so they should be used carefully. Constraints are basically rules restricting the values allowed in the columns and they define certain properties that data in a database must comply with. The purpose of constraints is to maintain the integrity of data in the database. The different ways of maintaining data integrity through constraints will be covered in this chapter.

Primary key indexes

As the name indicates, primary key indexes are the primary way to identify a record (tuple) in a table. Obviously, it cannot be null because a null (unknown) value cannot be used to identify a record. So, all RDBMSs prevent users from assigning a null value to the primary key. The primary key index is used to maintain uniqueness in a column. You can have only one primary key index on a table. It can be declared on multiple columns.

In the real world, for example, if you take the empid column of the emp table, you will be able to see a primary key index on that as no two employees can have the same empid value.

You can add a primary key index in two ways: One is while creating the table and the other, once the table has been created.

This is how you can add a primary key while creating a table:

```
CREATE TABLE emp(
  empid integer PRIMARY KEY,
  empname varchar,
  sal numeric);
```

And this is how you can add a primary key after a table has been created:

```
CREATE TABLE emp(
  empid integer,
  empname varchar,
  sal numeric);

ALTER TABLE emp ADD PRIMARY KEY(empid);
```

Irrespective of whether a primary key is created while creating a table or after the table is created, a unique index will be created implicitly. You can check the unique index through the following command:

```
postgres=# select * from pg_indexes where tablename='emp';
-[ RECORD 1 ]------------------------------------------------
schemaname | public
tablename  | emp
indexname  | emp_pkey
tablespace |
indexdef   | CREATE UNIQUE INDEX emp_pkey ON emp USING btree (empid)
```

Since it maintains uniqueness in the column, what happens if you try to INSERT a duplicate row or NULL values? Let's check it out:

```
postgres=# INSERT INTO emp VALUES(100, 'SCOTT', '10000.00');
INSERT 0 1
postgres=# INSERT INTO emp VALUES(100, 'ROBERT', '20000.00');
ERROR: duplicate key value violates unique constraint "emp_pkey"
DETAIL: Key (empid)=(100) already exists.
postgres=# INSERT INTO emp VALUES(null, 'ROBERT', '20000.00');
ERROR: null value in column "empid" violates not-null constraint
DETAIL: Failing row contains (null, ROBERT, 20000).
```

So, if empid is a duplicate value, the database throws an error; duplicate key violation due to unique constraint; if empid is null, the error is violates null constraint due to not-null constraint. A primary key is simply a combination of a unique and a not-null constraint.

Unique indexes

Like a primary key index, a unique index is also used to maintain uniqueness; however, it allows NULL values. The syntax is as follows:

```
CREATE TABLE emp(
  empid integer UNIQUE,
  empname varchar,
  sal numeric);

CREATE TABLE emp(
  empid integer,
  empname varchar,
  sal numeric,
  UNIQUE(empid));
```

This is what happens if you INSERT NULL values:

```
postgres=# INSERT INTO emp VALUES(100, 'SCOTT', '10000.00');
INSERT 0 1
postgres=# INSERT INTO emp VALUES(null, 'SCOTT', '10000.00');
INSERT 0 1
postgres=# INSERT INTO emp VALUES(null, 'SCOTT', '10000.00');
INSERT 0 1
```

As you see, it allows NULL values, and they are not even considered as duplicate values.

If a unique index is created on a column then there is no need for a standard index on the column. If you had one, it would just be a duplicate of the automatically created index. Currently, only B-tree indexes can be declared unique.

When a primary key is defined, PostgreSQL automatically creates a unique index. You can check it out using the following query:

```
postgres=# select * from pg_indexes where tablename ='emp';
-[ RECORD 1 ]----------------------------------------------
schemaname | public
tablename  | emp
indexname  | emp_empid_key
tablespace |
indexdef   | CREATE UNIQUE INDEX emp_empid_key ON emp USING btree
(empid)
```

B-tree indexes

Like most relational databases, PostgreSQL also supports B-tree indexes. Most RDBMS systems use B-tree as the default index type, unless something else is specified explicitly. Basically, this index keeps data stored in a tree (self-balancing) structure. It's the default index in PostgreSQL and fits in the most common situations.

The B-tree index can be used by an optimizer whenever the indexed column is used with a comparison operator, such as <, <=, =, >=, >, and LIKE or the ~ operator; however, LIKE or ~ will only be used if the pattern is a constant and anchored to the beginning of the string, for example, `my_col LIKE 'mystring%'` or `my_column ~ '^mystring'`, but not `my_column LIKE '%mystring'`.

Here is an example:

```
CREATE TABLE emp(
  empid integer,
  empname varchar,
  sal numeric);

INSERT INTO emp VALUES(100, 'scott', '10000.00');

INSERT INTO emp VALUES(100, 'clark', '20000.00');

INSERT INTO emp VALUES(100, 'david', '30000.00');

INSERT INTO emp VALUES(100, 'hans', '40000.00');
```

Create a B-tree index on the `empname` column:

```
CREATE INDEX emp_empid_idx ON emp(empid);
CREATE INDEX emp_name_idx ON emp(empname);
```

Here are the queries that use index:

```
postgres=# explain analyze SELECT * FROM emp WHERE empid=100;
                              QUERY PLAN
-----------------------------------------------------------------
Index Scan using emp_empid_idx on emp  (cost=0.13..4.15 rows=1  width=68)
(actual time=1.015..1.304 rows=4 loops=1)
Index Cond: (empid = 100)
Planning time: 0.496 ms
Execution time: 2.096 ms
postgres=# explain analyze SELECT * FROM emp WHERE empname LIKE  'da%';
                          QUERY PLAN
-----------------------------------------------------------------
Index Scan using emp_name_idx on emp  (cost=0.13..4.15 rows=1  width=68)
(actual time=0.956..0.959 rows=1 loops=1)
Index Cond: (((empname)::text >= 'david'::text) AND  ((empname)::text <
'david'::text))
Filter: ((empname)::text ~~ 'david%'::text)
Planning time: 2.285 ms
Execution time: 0.998 ms
```

Here is a query that cannot use index as `%` is used at the beginning of the string:

```
postgres=# explain analyze SELECT * FROM emp WHERE empname LIKE  '%david';
                          QUERY PLAN
-----------------------------------------------------------------
Seq Scan on emp  (cost=10000000000.00..10000000001.05 rows=1  width=68)
(actual time=0.014..0.015 rows=1 loops=1)
Filter: ((empname)::text ~~ '%david'::text)
Rows Removed by Filter: 3
Planning time: 0.099 ms
Execution time: 0.044 ms
```

Standard indexes

Indexes are primarily used to enhance database performance (though incorrect use can result in slower performance). An index can be created on multiple columns and multiple indexes can be created on one table. The syntax is as follows:

```
CREATE [ UNIQUE ] INDEX [ CONCURRENTLY ] [ name ] ON table_name [ USING
method ]
```

```
({ column_name | ( expression ) } [ COLLATE collation ] [ opclass ] [ ASC |
DESC ] [ NULLS { FIRST | LAST } ] [, ...])
[ WITH ( storage_parameter = value [, ... ] ) ]
[ TABLESPACE tablespace_name ]
[ WHERE predicate ]
```

PostgreSQL supports B-tree, hash, **Generalized Search Tree (GiST)**, SP-GiST, and **Generalized Inverted Index (GIN)**, which we will cover later in this chapter. If you do not specify any index type while creating it, creates a B-tree index as default.

Full text indexes

Let's talk about a document, for example a magazine article or an e-mail message. Normally, we use a text field to store a document. Searching for content within the document based on a matching pattern is called full text search. It is based on the @@ matching operator. You can check out http://www.postgresql.org/docs/current/static/textsearch-intro.html#TEXTSEARCH-MATCHING for more details.

Indexes on such full text fields are nothing but full text indexes. You can create a GIN index to speed up full text searches. We will cover GIN indexes later in this chapter. The syntax is as follows:

```
CREATE TABLE web_page(
  title text,
  heading text,
  body text);

CREATE INDEX web_page_title_body ON web_page USING
GIN(to_tsvector('english', body));
```

The preceding commands create a full text index on the body column of a web_page table.

Partial indexes

Partial indexes are one of the special features of PostgreSQL. Such indexes are not supported by many other RDBMSs. As the name suggests, if an index is created partially, which typically means the subset of a table, then it's a partial index. This subset is defined by a predicate (the WHERE clause). Its main purpose is to avoid common values. An index will essentially ignore a value that appears in a large fraction of a table's rows and the search will revert o a full table scan rather than an index scan. Therefore, indexing repeated values just wastes space and incurs the expense of the index updating without getting any performance benefit back at read time. So, common values should be avoided.

Let's take a common example, an emp table. Suppose you have a status column in an emp table that shows whether emp exists or not. In any case, you care about the current employees of an organization. In such cases, you can create a partial index in the status column by avoiding former employees.

Here is an example:

```
CREATE TABLE emp_table
  empid integer,
  empname varchar,
  status varchar);

INSERT INTO emp_table VALUES(100, 'scott', 'exists');

INSERT INTO emp_table VALUES(100, 'clark', 'exists');

INSERT INTO emp_table VALUES(100, 'david', 'not exists');

INSERT INTO emp_table VALUES(100, 'hans', 'not exists');
```

To create a partial index that suits our example, we will use the following query

```
CREATE INDEX emp_table_status_idx ON emp_table(status) WHERE  status NOT
IN('not exists');
```

Now, let's check the queries that can use the index and those that cannot.

A query that uses the index is as follows:

```
postgres=# explain analyze select * from emp_table where status='exists';
                         QUERY PLAN
-----------------------------------------------------------------
Index Scan using emp_table_status_idx on emp_table(cost=0.13..6.16 rows=2
width=17) (actual time=0.073..0.075 rows=2 loops=1)
Index Cond: ((status)::text = 'exists'::text)
```

A query that will not use the index is as follows:

```
postgres=# explain analyze select * from emp_table where
status='not exists';
                         QUERY PLAN
-----------------------------------------------------------------
Seq Scan on emp_table (cost=10000000000.00..10000000001.05 rows=1 width=17)
(actual time=0.013..0.014 rows=1 loops=1)
Filter: ((status)::text = 'not exists'::text)
Rows Removed by Filter: 3
```

Multicolumn indexes

PostgreSQL supports multicolumn indexes. If an index is defined simultaneously in more than one column then it is treated as a multicolumn index. The use case is pretty simple; for example, you have a website where you need a name and date of birth to fetch the required information, and then the query run against the database uses both fields as the predicate (the WHERE clause). In such scenarios, you can create an index in both the columns.

Here is an example:

```
CREATE TABLE get_info( name varchar, dob date, email varchar);
INSERT INTO get_info VALUES('scott', '1-1-1971',
'scott@example.com');

INSERT INTO get_info VALUES('clark', '1-10-1975',
'clark@example.com');

INSERT INTO get_info VALUES('david', '11-11-1971',
'david@somedomain.com');
INSERT INTO get_info VALUES('hans', '12-12-1971',
'hans@somedomain.com');
```

To create a multicolumn index, we will use the following command:

```
CREATE INDEX get_info_name_dob_idx ON get_info(name, dob);
```

A query that uses the index is as follows:

```
postgres=# explain analyze  SELECT * FROM get_info WHERE name='scott' AND
dob='1-1-1971';
                            QUERY PLAN
-----------------------------------------------------------------
Index Scan using get_info_name_dob_idx on get_info  (cost=0.13..4.15 rows=1
width=68) (actual time=0.029..0.031 rows=1  loops=1)
Index Cond: (((name)::text = 'scott'::text) AND (dob = '1971-01-
01'::date))
Planning time: 0.124 ms
Execution time: 0.096 ms
```

Hash indexes

These indexes can only be used with equality comparisons. So, an optimizer will consider using this index whenever an indexed column is used with the = operator.

Here is the syntax:

```
CREATE INDEX index_name ON table USING HASH (column);
```

Hash indexes are faster than B-tree as they should be used if the column in question is never intended to be scanned comparatively with < or > operators.

> The Hash indexes are not WAL-logged, so they might need to be rebuilt after a database crash, if there were any unwritten changes.

GIN and GiST indexes

GIN or GiST indexes are used for full text searches. GIN can only be created on the `tsvector` datatype columns and GIST on `tsvector` or `tsquery` database columns. The syntax is follows:

```
CREATE INDEX index_name ON table_name USING GIN (column_name);
CREATE INDEX index_name ON table_name USING GIST (column_name);
```

These indexes are useful when a column is queried for specific substrings on a regular basis; however, these are not mandatory.

What is the use case and when do we really need it? Let me give an example to explain. Suppose we have a requirement to implement simple search functionality for an application. Say, for example, we have to search through all users in the database. Also, let's assume that we have more than 10 million users currently stored in the database.

This search implementation requirement shows that we should be able to search using partial matches and multiple columns, for example, `first_name`, `last_name`. More precisely, if we have customers like Mitchell Johnson and John Smith, an input query of John should return for both customers. We can solve this problem using the GIN or GIST indexes.

Here is an example:

```
CREATE TABLE customers (first_name text, last_name text);
Create GIN/GiST index:
```

```
CREATE EXTENSION IF NOT EXISTS pg_trgm;
CREATE INDEX customers_search_idx_gin ON customers USING gin   (first_name
gin_trgm_ops, last_name gin_trgm_ops);
CREATE INDEX customers_search_idx_gist ON customers USING gist   (first_name
gist_trgm_ops, last_name gist_trgm_ops);
```

So, what is the difference between these two indexes? This is what the PostgreSQL documentation says:

- GiST is faster to update and build the index and is less accurate than GIN

GIN is slower to update and build the index but is more accurate. According to the documentation, the GiST index is lossy. This means that the index might produce false matches, and it is necessary to check the actual table row to eliminate such false matches (PostgreSQL does this automatically when needed).

Block Range Index (**BRIN**) indexes were introduced in PostgreSQL 9.5. BRIN indexes are designed to handle very large tables in which certain columns have some natural correlation with their physical location within the table. The syntax is follows:

```
CREATE INDEX index_name ON table_name USING brin(col);
```

Here is a good example: https://wiki.postgresql.org/wiki/What%27s_new_in_Postgre SQL_9.5#BRIN_Indexes.

Clustering on an index

PostgreSQL supports clustering a table using an index. CLUSTER is used to do that. What does it do? It reorganizes the table based on the index. Why do we need it? It can greatly increase performance when you query a range of index values or a single index value with multiple entries because the queried data is in one place on the disk.

The syntax is as follows:

```
CLUSTER [VERBOSE] table_name [ USING index_name ]
```

Here's an example of how to create a cluster and how it improves the performance:

```
CREATE TABLE table_cluster(
  id integer,
  name varchar);
INSERT INTO table_cluster VALUES(generate_series(1,10000000),
'test_name'||generate_series(1,10000000));
CREATE INDEX table_cluster_idx ON table_cluster(id);
```

Query the table in such way that the index is used and look at the execution time. The following is an example:

```
postgres=# EXPLAIN ANALYZE SELECT * FROM table_cluster WHERE id  BETWEEN
10000 AND 200000;
                         QUERY PLAN
----------------------------------------------------------------
Index Scan using table_cluster_idx on table_cluster  (cost=0.43..44955.39
rows=855991 width=19) (actual  time=1.741..535.026 rows=760004 loops=1)
Index Cond: ((id >= 10000) AND (id <= 200000))
Planning time: 5.241 ms
Execution time: 572.737 ms
```

Now, CLUSTER the table using index and query the table:

```
postgres=# CLUSTER table_cluster USING table_cluster_idx;
CLUSTERpostgres=# EXPLAIN ANALYZE SELECT * FROM table_cluster WHERE id
BETWEEN 10000 AND 200000
                         QUERY PLAN
----------------------------------------------------------------
Index Scan using table_cluster_idx on table_cluster  (cost=0.43..44955.39
rows=855991 width=19) (actual  time=1.777..272.387 rows=760004 loops=1)
Index Cond: ((id >= 10000) AND (id <= 200000))
Planning time: 0.283 ms
Execution time: 310.143 ms
```

If you can see, the query execution time reduced to almost 40%.

 Keep in mind that the CLUSTER operation takes an ACCESS EXCLUSIVE lock on the table, which typically means that it does not allow any other operation on the table while CLUSTER is running.

Foreign key constraints

Foreign key constraints maintain referential integrity between two related tables. They specify that values in a column of a table must match with some rows of another table.

Let's take one common example of the emp and dept table. We have to make sure that the emp table contains only valid deptno values, that can be found in the dept table:

```
CREATE TABLE dept(
deptno numeric PRIMARY KEY,
dname varchar,
loc varchar);
```

```
CREATE TABLE emp(
empno numeric PRIMARY KEY,
ename varchar,
job varchar,
mgr numeric,
hiredate date,
sal numeric,
comm numeric,
deptno numeric(2,0),
constraint fk_deptno foreign key (deptno) references dept
(deptno));
```

Let's try to INSERT some data in the emp table for which deptno does not exist in the dept table:

```
INSERT INTO dept VALUES(10, 'ACCOUNTING', 'NEW YORK');
INSERT INTO dept VALUES(20, 'RESEARCH', 'DALLAS');
```

We have a couple of deptno (10 and 20) in the dept table. As the foreign key constraint maintains referential integrity, it should not allow any deptno in the emp table other than 10 and 20. Let's try it using the following command:

```
INSERT INTO emp VALUES(7782, 'CLARK', 'MANAGER', 7839,to_date('9-
6-1981','dd-mm-yyyy'),2450, null, 40);
ERROR: insert or update on table "emp" violates foreign key  constraint
"fk_deptno" DETAIL:  Key (deptno)=(40) is not present  in table "dept".
```

It clearly throws an ERROR that, as deptno 40 is not in the dept table, it cannot be inserted in the emp table as well. In this way, we can maintain referential integrity by creating foreign key constraints.

Unique constraints

We create unique constraints to make sure that data contained in a column is unique among all rows in the table. The syntax is as follows:

```
CREATE TABLE example_1(
  col1 integer,
  col2 integer,
  col3 integer,
  UNIQUE(col1) );
```

It can be created on a group of columns as well. The syntax is as follows:

```
CREATE TABLE example_2(
  col1 integer,
```

```
    col2 integer,
    col3 integer,
    UNIQUE(col1, col2));
```

You can define a unique constraint even after the table is created, as shown in the following command:

```
ALTER TABLE example ADD CONSTRAINT example_col1_unique  UNIQUE(col1);
```

Adding this constraint will automatically create a B-tree index on the column.

 Please note that two null values are never considered equal in this comparison. That means though a unique constraint is defined, it is possible to store duplicate rows that contain a null value in at least one of the constrained columns. So, be careful when developing applications that are intended to be portable.

Now, let's try to insert duplicate values and see what error it throws:

```
INSERT INTO example_1 VALUES(1,2,1);

postgres=# INSERT INTO example
postgres-# VALUES(1,2,1);
ERROR: duplicate key value violates unique constraint
"example_col1_key"
DETAIL: Key (col1)=(1) already exists.
```

So, it clearly says, values already exist and cannot be inserted again. However, try inserting NULL values and see what happens:

```
postgres=# INSERT INTO example
postgres-# VALUES(null,1,1);
INSERT 0 1

postgres=# INSERT INTO example
postgres-# VALUES(null,1,1);
INSERT 0 1

postgres=# select * from example ;
col1 | col2 | col3
------+------+------
 | 1 | 1
 | 1 | 1
(2 rows)
```

So, as noted in the preceding example, a unique constraint does not consider null values as duplicates.

Check constraints

Check constraints allow you to specify that the value in a certain column must satisfy a Boolean (truth-value) expression. We use the CHECK keyword to define it. The syntax is as follows:

```
CREATE TABLE products(
  name varchar,
  product varchar,
  product_price numeric CHECK (product_price > 0));
```

In the preceding example, it makes sure that product_price is greater than 0. The previous example is a default value definition and a name will be given by the system; however, you can create check constraints with a separate name that clarifies error messages and allows you to refer to the constraint when you need to change it. Here is an example:

```
CREATE TABLE products(
  name varchar,
  product varchar,
  product_price numeric
  CONSTRAINT product_price_check CHECK (product_price > 1));
```

In the preceding definition, product_price_check is the name of the check constraint.

We can also define check constraints at table level, which is slightly different from column level. Here is an example:

```
CREATE TABLE products(
  name varchar,
  product varchar,
  product_price numeric CHECK (product_price > 0),
  discount_price numeric,
  CONSTRAINT discount_price_check CHECK (product_price >
  discount_price)
);
```

Let's test the check constraint by inserting some data:

```
INSERT INTO products VALUES('Pen', 'Stationary', '100.00', 0);
INSERT INTO products VALUES('Pen', 'Stationary', '-100.00',0);

ERROR:  new row for relation "products" violates check constraint
"products_check"
DETAIL:  Failing row contains (Pen, Stationary, -100.00, 0).
```

As per the column, the check constraint throws an error. However, it also has a table level constraint; let's check it by inserting some data:

```
INSERT INTO products VALUES('Pen', 'Stationary', '100.00',  '200.00');
ERROR:  new row for relation "products" violates check constraint
"discount_price_check"
DETAIL:  Failing row contains (Pen, Stationary, 100.00, 200.00).
```

If you look at the error, it clearly shows it is due to the "discount_price_check" constraint, which is defined at the table level.

NOT NULL constraints

As the name suggests, NOT NULL constraint simply specifies that a null value is not allowed. Let's take a look at an example:

```
CREATE TABLE products(
  name varchar,
  product varchar,
  product_price NOT NULL);
```

Let's test this constraint by inserting a null value:

```
INSERT INTO products VALUES('Pen', 'Stationary', null);
ERROR:  null value in column "product_price" violates not-null  constraint
DETAIL:  Failing row contains (Pen, Stationary, null).
```

PostgreSQL also supports NULL constraints. They should not be used in portable applications and are there for just compatibility as some other database systems have this. Here's an example:

```
CREATE TABLE products(
  name varchar NULL,
  product varchar,
  product_price integer NULL);
```

Exclusion constraints

This constraint specifies that if any two rows are compared on the specified column(s) or expression(s) using the specified operator(s), at least one of these operator comparisons will return false or null. Let's look at this example:

```
CREATE EXTENSION btree_gist;
CREATE TABLE example(
 name varchar,
 age integer,
 EXCLUDE USING gist
 (AGE WITH <>));
```

In the preceding example, we are enforcing that age has to match an already existing one. What happens if you try to insert a different age? Let's look at this example:

```
postgres=# INSERT INTO example VALUES ('scott', '26');
INSERT 0 1
postgres=# INSERT INTO example VALUES ('scott', '27');
ERROR:  conflicting key value violates exclusion constraint
"example_age_excl"
DETAIL:  Key (age)=(27) conflicts with existing key (age)=(26).
```

It throws an ERROR that the exclusion constraint is violated. Adding an exclusion constraint will automatically create an index of the type specified in the constraint declaration.

Summary

In this chapter, we looked at different types of indexes and constraints that PostgreSQL supports, how they are used in the real world with examples, and what happens if you violate a constraint. It not only helps you identify the right index for your data, but also improves the performance of the database. Every type of index or constraint has its own identification and need. Some indexes or constraints may not be portable to other RDBMSs, some may not be needed, or sometimes you might have chosen the wrong one for your needs. So be careful to choose the right one from which you get the benefit and one which satisfies your exact needs. In the next chapter, we will talk about the benefits of table partitioning in PostgreSQL and how to implement them. We will also cover managing partitions and alternate partitioning options.

7
Table Partitioning

In the last chapter, we talked about indexes and constraints in detail. It helped you to understand the purpose of indexes/constraints, and the best way we can use them in the real world. In this chapter, we are going to talk about table partitioning. We'll start with a basic introduction to partitioning, and will cover topics such as need for partitioning, the way it is done, and how exactly it helps. We will also discuss about the flow, that is, how it works so that you can have better control over it. You will learn how to manage table partitions once they are created, the kind of maintenance they require, and how to make the system get the best use out of it. We will also talk about types of partitioning that PostgreSQL supports, and alternative methods of partitioning. We will also discuss the impact if you do not partition a table.

Table partitioning

Partitioning is a feature in DBMS which segregates large amounts of data into multiple segments based on an attribute of a relation. Using this as a feature, we can perform operations effectively on large datasets. We can also go without partitioning the large datasets, but eventually we'll need to pay for performance as a result. The query response time and the amount of data it processes are inversely proportional. So, in short, the more data we have, the less performance we get (where performance is the actual time of query execution).

For example, consider we have a global business where we store all our global customers' information in our local database as follows:

```
CREATE TABLE customers
(id integer,
name varchar(126),
countrycode varchar(3),
contactnum text);
```

In the preceding table, we will store all our global customer details along with the `countrycode`. For demonstration purposes, I am going to use three-character country names, which are generated randomly from the following query:

```
postgres=# WITH stuff AS
(
    SELECT array['A', 'B', 'C', 'D', 'E', 'F', 'G', 'H'] as names,
    array['USA', 'UK', 'UAE', 'IND', 'GER', 'RUS'] AS cnames)
INSERT INTO customers
SELECT Generate_series(1, 1000) id,
names[(random()*100)::int%8+1] cname,
cnames[(random()*100)::int%6+1] countrycode,
ltrim(round(random()::numeric, 10)::text, '0.') contactnumber
FROM stuff;
INSERT 0 1000
```

In the preceding query, we took an array of customer and country names, which we are going to choose randomly to populate into our `customers` table; we then populated our table with `1000` entries. As an ad hoc reporting request, let's assume that we need to count the number of customers we have in `'USA'`, `'UK'`, and `'IND'`. Here is the query for the request:

We enable `timing` at psql client, which gives us the total query execution followed by the query result.

```
postgres=# \timing
Timing is on.
postgres=# SELECT COUNT(*), countrycode FROM customers WHERE countrycode IN
('USA', 'UK', 'IND') GROUP BY countrycode;
count | countrycode
------+-------
  167 | UK
  171 | IND
  154 | USA
Time: 9.202 ms
```

From the preceding result, we see that the query execution takes `9.202 ms` to operate on `1000` records. Let's push more records into the table, and see the response time. In the following request, I push 10 times the current record count.

Now, let's execute our ad hoc request, and see the response time.

```
postgres=# SELECT COUNT(*), countrycode FROM customers WHERE   countrycode
IN ('USA', 'UK', 'IND') GROUP BY countrycode;
count | countrycode
------+-------
```

```
  1858 | UK
  1810 | IND
  1930 | UAE
Time: 9.661 ms
```

From the preceding results, it seems we paid 0.459 ms extra time for the same query, on a large dataset. Let's increase the dataset by 10 times the current record count, and see the response time for the same query:

```
postgres=# SELECT COUNT(*), countrycode FROM customers WHERE   countrycode
IN ('USA', 'UK', 'IND') GROUP BY countrycode;
count | countrycode
------+---------
16962 | UK
16382 | USA
16925 | IND
(3 rows)
Time: 70.994 ms
```

From the preceding examples, we can see that the query response time is inversely proportional to the dataset. So first let's try to optimize the query, which will improve the query response time without using the partition.

Let's look at the query execution plan:

```
postgres=# EXPLAIN ANALYZE SELECT COUNT(*), countrycode FROM  customers
WHERE countrycode IN ('USA', 'UK', 'IND') GROUP BY  countrycode;
                            QUERY PLAN
-----------------------------------------------------------------
HashAggregate  (cost=2262.65..2262.69 rows=4 width=3) (actual
time=78.162..78.163 rows=3 loops=1)
Group Key: countrycode
->  Seq Scan on customers  (cost=0.00..2012.00 rows=50130 width=3)  (actual
time=0.017..50.113 rows=50269 loops=1)
Filter: ((countrycode)::text = ANY ('{USA,UK,IND}'::text[]))
Rows Removed by Filter: 49731
Planning time: 0.195 ms
Execution time: 78.227 ms
(7 rows)
Time: 79.157 ms
```

From the preceding plan, we see that our predicate column (countrycode) is not indexed. That is the reason it went for a sequential scan. Let's create an index and see the plan:

```
postgres=# CREATE INDEX CONCURRENTLY countrycode_idx ON
customers(countrycode);
CREATE INDEX
Time: 390.520 ms
```

```
postgres=# EXPLAIN ANALYZE SELECT COUNT(*), countrycode FROM  customers
WHERE countrycode IN ('USA', 'UK', 'IND') GROUP BY  countrycode;
                            QUERY PLAN
-------------------------------------------------------------------
HashAggregate  (cost=2262.65..2262.69 rows=4 width=3) (actual
time=74.823..74.823 rows=3 loops=1)
Group Key: countrycode
->  Seq Scan on customers  (cost=0.00..2012.00 rows=50130 width=3)   (actual
time=0.018..47.365 rows=50269 loops=1)
Filter: ((countrycode)::text = ANY ('{USA,UK,IND}'::text[]))
Rows Removed by Filter: 49731
Planning time: 0.378 ms
Execution time: 74.883 ms
(7 rows)
Time: 75.866 ms
```

It seems our assumption is incorrect. Even after creating the index on the required predicate column, our query still takes the sequential scan. This is the expected behavior when a query tries to fetch more than 50% of the table;the optimizer skips the index scan in that case. If you observe the previous execution plan, we see `rows=50269`, which is 50% of the actual table count. That is the reason our index did not get picked up. Here I inserted six country codes randomly, out of which I selected three country codes. It means that we selected 50% of the actual table.

So let's try to eliminate one `countrycode` from the predicate, and see if the plan takes the created index:

```
postgres=# EXPLAIN ANALYZE SELECT COUNT(*), countrycode FROM customers
WHERE countrycode IN ('USA', 'UK') GROUP BY countrycode;
                            QUERY PLAN
-------------------------------------------------------------------
HashAggregate  (cost=1794.58..1794.60 rows=2 width=3) (actual
time=39.266..39.267 rows=2 loops=1)
Group Key: countrycode
->  Bitmap Heap Scan on customers  (cost=574.71..1628.04  rows=33307
width=3) (actual time=11.880..20.284 rows=33344  loops=1)
Recheck Cond: ((countrycode)::text = ANY ('{USA,UK}'::text[]))
Heap Blocks: exact=637
-> Bitmap Index Scan on countrycode_idx (cost=0.00..566.38  rows=33307
width=0) (actual time=11.724..11.724 rows=33344  loops=1)
Index Cond: ((countrycode)::text = ANY ('{USA,UK}'::text[]))
Planning time: 0.167 ms
Execution time: 39.343 ms
(9 rows)
Time: 40.007 ms
```

Yeah, now it works. Moreover, we reduced the query response time to half by creating the index on the required predicate column. Here the query fetches less than 50% of the actual record set.

In the preceding example, we reduced the query response time to some extent by creating the required index. However, our global business will not stop with a certain number of clients. Business needs to scale and get more customers. So let's insert more records into the `customers` table, and see the query response time.

```
postgres=# SELECT COUNT(*) FROM customers;
count
---------
3000000
(1 row)
Time: 926.910 ms
postgres=# EXPLAIN ANALYZE SELECT COUNT(*), countrycode FROM  customers
WHERE countrycode IN ('USA', 'UK') GROUP BY countrycode;
                              QUERY PLAN
-----------------------------------------------------------------
GroupAggregate  (cost=0.43..106932.53 rows=3 width=3) (actual
time=492.174..930.943 rows=2 loops=1)
Group Key: countrycode
->  Index Only Scan using countrycode_idx on customers
(cost=0.43..101860.00 rows=1014500 width=3) (actual  time=0.117..697.074
rows=1004893 loops=1)
Index Cond: (countrycode = ANY ('{USA,UK}'::text[]))
Heap Fetches: 1004893
Planning time: 0.350 ms
Execution time: 931.001 ms
(7 rows)
Time: 932.133 ms
```

In the preceding example, the index scan helps us to reduce the query response time. However, if the table keeps on growing like this, even index scans might not help us after a certain point.

So what is the best solution to handle this kind of large data sets? As of now, the solution to achieve better performance is **partitioning**. You might wonder, "How do we partition a table, and how we can manage the partitions?". Let's discuss this in more detail.

Partition implementation

What does actually happen when we implement partitions on any table?

- Does Postgres create a different storage for the partition?
- Is this partition object similar to objects like an index or a view?
- Is this a mechanism that internally segregates table data into multiple chunks?

To answer all these questions, partitioning a table is nothing but creating a separate table called a child table for each partition. Child tables do not have any special characteristics, as they are completely similar to normal tables. The original table on which we create a partition is called the parent table. Let's see more details about parent and child tables in further discussions.

Before implementing partitions on any table, we have to take a decision on which column of the table we need to create partitions. Also, we need to understand the column's data type too.

So how to choose a column for partitioning?

In our table structure, we have columns like `id`, `name`, `countrycode`, and `contactnum`. And we need to choose a column on which to a create partition, which will improve our query response time. In general, we need to choose a column whose values are more repetitive than any other column. For example, the `id`, `name`, and `contactnum` columns will have fewer repetitive values than `countrycode`. And the data type of the `countrycode` is text.

As I mentioned earlier, before creating any partition we need to choose a proper column in the table along with its data type. Here, we chose `countrycode` as our partitioning column since it has more duplicate values than other columns.

So, we are finally ready to do partitioning of a table. As mentioned previously, we need to create partitions on the parent table.

So, let's create a parent table first, and then will create child (partition) tables:

```
postgres=# CREATE TABLE IF NOT EXISTS customers
(id int, name varchar(126),
countrycode varchar(3),
contactnum text);
```

You might've noticed that the syntax for creation of a parent table is similar to that of our regular tables. Yes, you are correct. Regular tables become parent tables when we partition them.

Now, let's create child tables for the parent table, and partition the table on each country code. We have six country codes, so create one child table for each country code in the parent table, which will be six in total, and suffix the country code to the table name for easy understanding.

This is done as follows:

```
CREATE TABLE customers_USA(CHECK (countrycode='USA'))  INHERITS(customers);
CREATE TABLE customers_UK(CHECK (countrycode='UK'))  INHERITS(customers);
CREATE TABLE customers_UAE(CHECK (countrycode='UAE'))  INHERITS(customers);
CREATE TABLE customers_IND(CHECK (countrycode='IND'))  INHERITS(customers);
CREATE TABLE customers_GER(CHECK (countrycode='GER'))  INHERITS(customers);
CREATE TABLE customers_RUS(CHECK (countrycode='RUS'))  INHERITS(customers);
```

Now look at the difference in syntax for creation of the child tables. While creating the child tables, we have used the INHERITS table feature, which will automatically inherit the given table's columns along with its modifiers like not null, and default properties.

Also, we have added an additional data consistency CHECK constraint, which makes sure that the created child table will only allow the respective country code values.

We can use psql's meta command(\d+) to see all the child tables of a partitioned table, as follows:

```
postgres=# \d+ customers
Table "public.customers"
Column | Type | Modifiers | Storage | Stats target | Description
-------+------+-----------+---------+--------------+--------------
id | integer |   | plain |   |
name | character varying(126) |   | extended |   |
countrycode | character varying(3) |   | extended |   |
contactnum  | text |   | extended |   |
Child tables: customers_ger,
customers_ind,
customers_rus,
customers_uae,
customers_uk,
customers_usa
```

Or, we can also use pg_inherits table, to get a child's information:

```
postgres=# SELECT inhrelid::regclass, inhparent::regclass from  pg_inherits
WHERE inhparent::regclass='customers'::regclass;
     inhrelid | inhparent
--------------+-----------
customers_usa | customers
customers_uk  | customers
```

```
customers_uae | customers
customers_ind | customers
customers_ger | customers
customers_rus | customers
```

Now, you might have another question like "How is my application going to communicate with the child tables?" Actually, your application has no need to know what all the child tables for the given partitioned table are, as your application only deals with the parent table.

All application DML operations will be diverted to the corresponding child table with the help of the INHERITS feature along with the before insert trigger on the parent table.

So let's create a before insert trigger on the parent table, and see how the parent table handles the incoming DML operations:

```
CREATE OR REPLACE FUNCTION customers_before_insert_trig_func() RETURNS
trigger AS
$$
BEGIN

IF (NEW.countrycode='USA') THEN
  INSERT INTO customers_usa VALUES(NEW.*);
ELSIF (NEW.countrycode='UK') THEN
  INSERT INTO customers_uk VALUES(NEW.*);
ELSIF (NEW.countrycode='IND') THEN
  INSERT INTO customers_ind VALUES(NEW.*);
ELSIF (NEW.countrycode='GER') THEN
  INSERT INTO customers_GER VALUES(NEW.*);
ELSIF (NEW.countrycode='UAE') THEN
  INSERT INTO customers_uae VALUES(NEW.*);
ELSIF (NEW.countrycode='RUS') THEN
  INSERT INTO customers_rus VALUES(NEW.*);
ELSE
  --Unknown country code, we got as an input.
  --Here, we can either RAISE ERROR or
  --We can store the unknown country code on some other child table
  RAISE EXCEPTION 'Unknown country code we got';
END IF;
RETURN NULL;
END;
$$ LANGUAGE PLPGSQL;

CREATE TRIGGER customers_ins_trig before INSERT ON customers FOR each row
EXECUTE PROCEDURE
customers_before_insert_trig_func();
```

From the preceding trigger function, we can see that an explicit INSERT operation is happening on the corresponding child table, based on the country codes. In this way, we can handle our INSERT operation on the parent table.

Now let's insert a few random records, and see how it goes:

```
postgres=# WITH stuff AS(
   SELECT array['A', 'B', 'C', 'D', 'E', 'F', 'G', 'H']  as names,
   array['USA', 'UK', 'UAE', 'IND', 'GER', 'RUS'] AS cnames)
INSERT INTO customers
SELECT Generate_series(1, 1000) id,
names[(random()*100)::int%8+1] cname,
cnames[(random()*100)::int%6+1] countrycode,
ltrim(round(random()::numeric, 10)::text, '0.') contactnumber
FROM stuff;
INSERT 0 0
```

You might wonder how we got INSERT 0 0 even though we inserted 1000 records into the database. Let's check the count of the parent table:

```
postgres=# SELECT COUNT(*) FROM customers;
count
-------
1000
(1 row)
```

We have 1000 records; however, our actual INSERT operation returned inserted records. The reason behind this discrepancy is the TRIGGER function. Our trigger function diverts the incoming INSERT into its corresponding child table, and returns INSERT 0 0 as a result to the parent table. So indirectly, we are inserting records into child tables and not into the parent table. That's the reason our INSERT returned 0.

Now, you might have a questions like, "Who cares if the records are inserted into the parent or the child?" and "What happens if we get INSERT 0 when we insert a record into the master?" To answer these questions, we need to discuss more about application implementation. If your application has a method called reportStatus based on the number of records we insert into a table, it always fails in this kind of a partitioning approach. For example, consider the Java hibernate API. This API always returns the number of records it inserts/updates/deletes in a table. If hibernate fails to get the number of records it expects, we will get the following ERROR message in our application logs:

```
ERROR:
org.hibernate.StaleStateException: Batch update returned  unexpected row
count from update [0]; actual row count: 0;  expected: 1
```

The preceding ERROR message is from the application, and it is not a db error message. To handle these kinds of ERROR messages in hibernate, we need to use SQLInsert annotations as follows:

```
@SQLInsert(
    sql="<INSERT Statement>",
    check=ResultCheckStyle.NONE)
```

This is one of the side-effects of using partitions in PostgreSQL, and we need to handle this carefully.

We actually implemented partitions to solve the performance problem. Let's see the response time for the same record count with partitioning.

We have a total of three million records in a partitioned table:

```
postgres=# SELECT COUNT(*) FROM customers;
count
--------
3000000
(1 row)
Time: 867.000 ms
```

Let's execute the same query for our partitioned table:

```
postgres=# EXPLAIN ANALYZE SELECT COUNT(*), countrycode FROM  customers
WHERE countrycode IN ('USA', 'UK') GROUP BY countrycode;
                        QUERY PLAN
-------------------------------------------------------------------
HashAggregate  (cost=23978.96..23980.96 rows=200 width=3) (actual
time=1074.627..1074.629 rows=2 loops=1)
Group Key: customers.countrycode
-> Append  (cost=0.00..18956.11 rows=1004570 width=3) (actual
time=0.020..604.916 rows=1004569 loops=1)
-> Seq Scan on customers  (cost=0.00..0.00 rows=1 width=16)  (actual
time=0.002..0.002 rows=0 loops=1)
Filter: ((countrycode)::text = ANY ('{USA,UK}'::text[]))
-> Seq Scan on customers_usa  (cost=0.00..9334.16 rows=494653  width=4)
(actual time=0.017..216.141 rows=494653 loops=1)
Filter: ((countrycode)::text = ANY ('{USA,UK}'::text[]))
-> Seq Scan on customers_uk  (cost=0.00..9621.95 rows=509916  width=3)
(actual time=0.012..261.808 rows=509916 loops=1)
Filter: ((countrycode)::text = ANY ('{USA,UK}'::text[]))
Planning time: 0.619 ms
Execution time: 1074.712 ms
(11 rows)
```

Let's see the same plan on the table that is not partitioned:

```
EXPLAIN ANALYZE SELECT COUNT(*), countrycode FROM customers WHERE
countrycode IN ('USA', 'UK') GROUP BY countrycode;
                        QUERY PLAN
-----------------------------------------------------------------
HashAggregate  (cost=24624.81..24624.83 rows=2 width=16) (actual
time=1975.003..1975.003 rows=2 loops=1)
Group Key: countrycode
-> Seq Scan on customers  (cost=0.00..24602.84 rows=4395 width=16)  (actual
time=0.039..1471.151 rows=1004569 loops=1)
Filter: ((countrycode)::text = ANY ('{USA,UK}'::text[]))
Rows Removed by Filter: 1995431
Planning time: 0.222 ms
Execution time: 1975.078 ms
(7 rows)
```

In the preceding two plans, we get better performance from the first plan. If you look at the second plan, the query scanned all of the three million records to fetch the 'USA', and 'UK' entries from the table, whereas in the first plan it only scanned the customers_usa and customers_uk child tables. So in plan 2, postgres only scanned the required child tables rather than scanning them all.

Now you might have a question like, "How does Postgres know which child tables it needs to scan for retrieval?" We will discuss about this in our next topic on **constraint_exclusion**, and for now, just keep this question in abeyance.

Partitioning types

In our example, we created partitioning on the countries table using the countrycode column. Here, the data type of the countrycode attribute is TEXT. On TEXT data types, we can have only a certain kind of partition. Based on the column's data type, we can create different kinds of partitions, like the following:

List partition

This is what we created for the countries table, but in the mentioned examples we have only one value in the list. We can also do partitioning of the customers table as follows where we will store more countries into a single child table:

```
CREATE TABLE customers_APAC (CHECK(countrycode IN ('CHI', 'IND', 'JAP',
'THA')))  INHERITS(customers);
```

Using the preceding approach, we are going to store multiple information on Asian countries into a single child table. We also need to update the trigger body as follows:

```
CREATE OR REPLACE FUNCTION customers_before_insert_trig_func()   RETURNS
trigger AS
...
...
IF (NEW.countrycode IN ('CHI', 'IND', 'JAP', 'THA') ) THEN
INSERT INTO customers_apac VALUES(NEW.*);
...
...
LANGUAGE PLPGSQL;
```

Once we create the preceding list partition, all records that have the mentioned entries will be directed to the respective child table.

- **Range partition**: We can create child tables based on some range values. To demonstrate this range partition, let's assume that we store all the DB/App logs into the database for further processing.

- Parent table:

    ```
    CREATE TABLE LOGS
    (id INT,
    recorded_date DATE,
    logmsg TEXT);
    ```

- Child tables are created as follows:

    ```
    CREATE TABLE LOGS_2015JAN(CHECK(recorded_date>='2015-01-01'
    AND recorded_date<'2015-02-01')) INHERITS(LOGS);
    CREATE TABLE LOGS_2015FEB(CHECK(recorded_date>='2015-02-01'
    AND recorded_date<'2015-03-01')) INHERITS(LOGS);
    ...
    ...
    CREATE TABLE LOGS_2015DEC(CHECK(recorded_date>='2015-12-01'
    AND recorded_date<'2016-01-01')) INHERITS(LOGS);
    ```

- Also, we need to create a trigger on the parent table with range conditions as follows:

    ```
    CREATE OR REPLACE FUNCTION logs_before_insert_trig_func()
    RETURNS trigger AS
    ...
    ...
    IF (NEW.recorded_date>='2015-01-01' AND
    recorded_date<'2015- 02-01')THEN
    ```

```
INSERT INTO logs_2015jan VALUES(NEW.*);
. . .
. . .
LANGUAGE PLPGSQL;
```

Once we create this range partition, all the records that fall into the given range will be directed to the respective child table:

 In PostgreSQL, we only have list and range partitions.

Managing partitions

Our main motive in creating partitions is to handle large datasets. In our previous example, the customers partitioned table, we created six child partitions based on countrycode. In the future, if we want to add another countrycode to the existing table, or if we want to delete a specific countrycode data from the customers table, it will require different management operations.

Adding a new partition

First we will discuss how to embed a new child table into an existing partition. Let's consider adding a new countrycode 'JAP'.

Create a new child table like the other child tables we created earlier:

```
CREATE TABLE customers_jap(CHECK(countrycode='JAP'))  INHERITS(customers);
```

Add a new ELSIF section to the parent's insert trigger, as follows:

```
CREATE OR REPLACE FUNCTION customers_before_insert_trig_func()  RETURNS
trigger AS
. . .
. . .
ELSIF(countrycode='JAP') THEN
INSERT INTO customers_jap VALUES(NEW.*);
LANGUAGE PLPGSQL;
```

Creating a child table for every country code seems fine. However, changing the trigger definition each time for every new addition would not be a proper solution. If we make our trigger code a bit dynamic, that will make our partition management somewhat easier.

Here is a dynamic trigger function code that automatically INSERT into child tables:

```
CREATE OR REPLACE FUNCTION  public.customers_before_insert_trig_func()
RETURNS trigger AS
$$
BEGIN
EXECUTE 'INSERT INTO customers_'||NEW.countrycode||' VALUES  ($1.*)' USING
NEW;
RETURN NULL;
END
$$
LANGUAGE plpgsql;
```

You'll see that, by suffixing the country code to the INSERT statement, the preceding sample code automatically detects the child partition name.

Purging an old partition

To purge an existing child table from the partition, we have to do the following operations on the parent table:

- Remove the child table from inheritance
- Adjust the trigger function code as per purging

To remove a child table from inheritance, we have to execute the following ALTER command on the child table.

```
postgres=# ALTER TABLE customers_jap NO INHERIT customers;
ALTER TABLE
```

Once we remove the child table from inheritance, it will not be part of all its parent table's operations.

After this, we can either truncate or drop the child table. Also, we have to take care of the parent table's trigger functionality. If it's a dynamic trigger function, then we do not need to adjust anything in the trigger functionality. If it's not dynamic, then we have to remove the INSERT ELSIF section from the actual trigger body.

We can also automate partitioning maintenance operations by creating our own scripts and scheduling them. As PostgreSQL is open source, we will need more extensions to automate these maintenance operations. `pg_partman`, which is an extension in PostgreSQL, takes care of all our maintenance operations easily. We can also schedule our maintenance operations using `pg_partman`. You can find more details about this extension at `https://github.com/keithf4/pg_partman`.

Alternate partitioning methods

As of now, we created partitions on a table as follows:

- Creating a set of child tables, and making them inherit from the parent table
- Adding a before insert trigger function on the parent table

In PostgreSQL, we have other different approaches to create partitioning tables. Let's discuss about other alternative methods too.

Method 1

As an alternative to creating triggers on parent table and `INHERITS` to child tables, we can use rules.

And, as an alternative to the parent table, we can use a view with a union of all individual tables along with the `INSTEAD OF` triggers.

Let's make our example compatible with `RULE` in the next code. Let's disable the trigger on the parent table such that it is not invoked during the `INSERT` operations, and let `RULE` take care of that.

```
postgres=# ALTER TABLE customers DISABLE trigger  customers_ins_trig;
postgres=# CREATE RULE cutomers_usa_rule AS ON INSERT TO customers  WHERE
countrycode = 'USA'
DO INSTEAD INSERT INTO customers_usa VALUES(NEW.*);
. . .
. . .
. . .
postgres=# CREATE RULE cutomers_rus_rule AS ON INSERT TO customers  WHERE
countrycode = 'RUS'
DO INSTEAD INSERT INTO customers_rus VALUES(NEW.*);
```

In PostgreSQL, RULE works similarly to triggers; however, RULE gets executed only BEFORE an event occurs. RULE is an alternative action to the actual db operation. Also, RULE has some limitations; for example, the COPY statement skips rules on any table during bulk inserting, which is not the case with triggers. So it is always recommended to go with TRIGGER rather than RULE.

Method 2

Now we will discuss another method to create partitions. For this method, we need to create individual child tables as follows:

```
postgres=# CREATE TABLE customers_usa(id int, name varchar(126),
countrycode varchar(3), contactnum text);
postgres=# CREATE TABLE customers_uk(id int, name varchar(126),
countrycode varchar(3), contactnum text);
postgres=# CREATE TABLE customers_uae(id int, name varchar(126),
countrycode varchar(3), contactnum text);
postgres=# CREATE TABLE customers_ind(id int, name varchar(126),
countrycode varchar(3), contactnum text);
postgres=# CREATE TABLE customers_ger(id int, name varchar(126),
countrycode varchar(3), contactnum text);
postgres=# CREATE TABLE customers_rus(id int, name varchar(126),
countrycode varchar(3), contactnum text);
```

Next we need to create a parent table for these child tables. In the previous approaches, we created a table and all the child tables inherited that parent table. However, in this approach, we are going to use a VIEW as a parent table to the child tables, and an INSTEAD OF trigger to navigate the DML statements to the respective child table. Here we can not use RULE with VIEW in place of the INSTEAD OF trigger, since it will not provide the required functionality that we are looking for.

Here is the parent table(view) for the child tables:

```
postgres=# CREATE VIEW v_customers AS SELECT * FROM customers_usa
UNION ALL
SELECT * FROM customers_uk
UNION ALL
SELECT * FROM customers_uae
UNION ALL
SELECT * FROM customers_ind
UNION ALL
SELECT * FROM customers_ger
UNION ALL
SELECT * FROM customers_rus ;
```

The following is the trigger body that navigates DML operations on a VIEW into its child tables:

```
CREATE OR REPLACE FUNCTION  public.customers_before_insert_trig_func()
RETURNS trigger AS
$$
BEGIN
IF TG_OP='INSERT' THEN
  EXECUTE 'INSERT INTO customers_'||NEW.countrycode||' VALUES
  ($1.*)' USING NEW;
ELSIF TG_OP='DELETE' THEN
  EXECUTE 'DELETE FROM customers_'||OLD.countrycode||' WHERE id=$1
  and name=$2 and contactnum=$3' USING OLD.id, OLD.name,
  OLD.contactnum;
ELSIF TG_OP='UPDATE' THEN
  EXECUTE 'UPDATE customers_'||OLD.countrycode||' SET id=$1,
  name=$2, contactnum=$3 WHERE id=$4 and name=$5 and contactnum=$6'
  USING NEW.id, NEW.name, NEW.contactnum, OLD.id, OLD.name,
  OLD.contactnum;
END IF;
RETURN NULL;
END
$$
LANGUAGE plpgsql;
```

The INSTEAD OF trigger on the view is defined as follows:

```
CREATE TRIGGER cutomer_trig
INSTEAD OF INSERT OR UPDATE OR DELETE ON v_customers
FOR EACH ROW
EXECUTE PROCEDURE customers_before_insert_trig_func();
```

Now let's try to do some simple operations:

```
postgres=# INSERT INTO customers VALUES(1, 'A', 'USA', '1');
INSERT 0 0
postgres=# UPDATE customers SET name = 'B' WHERE name ='A';
UPDATE 0
postgres=# DELETE FROM customers;
DELETE 0
```

It seems our DML operations are working fine on VIEW. Now let's try any DDL operation:

```
postgres=# truncate v_customers;
ERROR:  "customers" is not a table
```

In the preceding case, it fails and gives an ERROR saying that customers is not a table.

Now let's try to do BULK insert via the COPY statement.

```
postgress=# COPY customers FROM STDIN;
>> 1, 'A', 'USA', 'A'
>> \.
ERROR: cannot copy to view "customers"
```

From the preceding two alternative methods, we see that partition creation and its maintenance are slightly more difficult than the actual implementation. It is also recommended to use the direct partitioning approach rather than these alternatives, since these alternative methods have their own drawbacks.

Constraint exclusion

We use partitioning to achieve better performance on big datasets, and **constraint exclusion** plays a vital role in doing this. Let's put partitioning aside for now, and see what constraint exclusion is and how it helps to improve performance on regular tables.

Constraint exclusion is a hint to the optimizer to generate the best execution plan.

To demonstrate this, let's create a simple table as follows:

```
postgres=# CREATE TABLE testing(t CHAR(1) CHECK(t='A'));
CREATE TABLE
postgres=# INSERT INTO testing VALUES('A');
INSERT 0 1
```

Now let's disable CONSTRAINT_EXCLUSION, and see the plan:

```
postgres=# SET CONSTRAINT_EXCLUSION TO OFF;
SET
```

The preceding table, testing, only accepts the character 'A' as an input into the table. Now, if you insert a character 'Z', it will throw an exception like this:

```
postgres=# INSERT INTO testing VALUES('Z');
ERROR:  new row for relation "testing" violates check constraint
"testing_t_check"
DETAIL:  Failing row contains (Z).
```

However, what happens if I try to SELECT an invalid record? Does it throw any ERROR message. No, it does not, right? Rather, it will scan the whole table for the record 'z', and finally return zero records, like this:

```
postgres=# EXPLAIN ANALYZE SELECT * FROM testing WHERE t='Z';
                          QUERY PLAN
-----------------------------------------------------------------
Seq Scan on testing  (cost=0.00..38.25 rows=11 width=8) (actual
time=0.020..0.020 rows=0 loops=1)
Filter: (t = 'Z'::bpchar)
Rows Removed by Filter: 1
Planning time: 0.074 ms
Execution time: 0.053 ms
(5 rows)
```

Now let's enable CONSTRAINT_EXCLUSION, and see the plan again:

```
postgres=# SET CONSTRAINT_EXCLUSION TO ON;
SET
postgres=# EXPLAIN ANALYZE SELECT * FROM testing WHERE t='Z';
                          QUERY PLAN
-----------------------------------------------------------------
Result  (cost=0.00..0.01 rows=1 width=0) (actual time=0.001..0.001  rows=0
loops=1)
One-Time Filter: false
Planning time: 0.192 ms
Execution time: 0.016 ms
(4 rows)
```

Now if you see the preceding plan, there is no Seq Scan happened on the table to fetch 'z' records. In this case, the optimizer is smart enough to identify whether it needs to scan the whole table or not.

Also, enabling this parameter will increase the planning time, but the actual execution time will be reduced if the given predicate doesn't match the constraints.

This parameter accepts three values as an input:

- **partition (Default)**: Only applicable for partitioned tables
- **On**: Applicable for all tables including temp tables
- **Off**: If we query the actual partitioned table customers, we see that only the required partitioned tables will be scanned rather than all tables

The following is another sample that only scans the `customers` table, which is the parent, and `customers_ind`, which is a partitioned table, as per our predicate:

```
postgres=# EXPLAIN ANALYZE SELECT * FROM customers WHERE   countrycode =
'IND';
                          QUERY PLAN
---------------------------------------------------------------
Append (cost=0.00..9633.69 rows=510536 width=20) (actual
time=0.292..364.390 rows=510535 loops=1)
-> Seq Scan on customers  (cost=0.00..0.00 rows=1 width=322)   (actual
time=0.002..0.002 rows=0 loops=1)
Filter: ((countrycode)::text = 'IND'::text)
-> Seq Scan on customers_ind  (cost=0.00..9633.69 rows=510535  width=20)
(actual time=0.289..299.973 rows=510535 loops=1)
Filter: ((countrycode)::text = 'IND'::text)
Planning time: 134.596 ms
Execution time: 394.600 ms
(7 rows)
```

In the preceding partitioning, we created child tables with the CHECK constraints. That is the reason why, when we queried the parent table, the constraint_exclusion hint was applied on the corresponding child tables, and only the required tables were scanned instead of all tables.

We can also experiment by switching off that parameter, which will result in scanning all the child tables.

Horizontal partitioning

So far, we've discussed creating partitions in a single database, and storing all the child tables in local machines.

Now if we can store those child tables in other databases, either in localhost or remote host, that will definitely give better performance than storing all the child tables in a single database. To achieve this good performance, we have two approaches, which are:

- PL/Proxy
- PostgreSQL 9.5 feature, foreign inheritance

PL/Proxy

This Postgres PL extension from Skype, scales a single database into multiple instances. PL/Proxy needs a function-based API for database operations. That is, we need a function to retrieve data, and another function for other DML operations.

The way PL/Proxy works is like a central db server which navigates the db operations to the different instances. Here, the navigation will be calculated using the `hashtext()` function and the number of partitions we have. Also, PL/Proxy works on a power of 2 number of partitions only. That is, we need to have $2^{\wedge}(N)$ number of partitions to configure PL/Proxy.

To configure this extension in db, please refer to `https://plproxy.github.io/tutorial.html`.

Consider our example of the `customers` table that we partitioned on the basis of `countrycode`. In all the examples related to this `customers` table, we demonstrated list partitioning. However, we cannot configure list/range partitioning using Pl/Proxy. PL/Proxy only supports hash-based partitioning like this:

```
postgres=# WITH countries as (SELECT UNNEST(ARRAY['USA', 'UK',  'IND',
'GER', 'RUS', 'UAE', 'JAP', 'CHI']) countrycode)
SELECT hashtext(countrycode) & 7 partnumber, countrycode FROM  countries;
partnumber | countrycode
-----------+------------
         7 | USA
         2 | UK
         3 | IND
         7 | GER
         7 | RUS
         3 | UAE
         5 | JAP
         0 | CHI
(8 rows)
```

Based on the preceding `hashtext(countrycode)` and *((Number of partitions)-1)* calculation, PL/Proxy decides which partition it needs to get the data from, or on which partition it needs to execute DMLoperations. We need to embed this calculation in the PL/Proxy function.

In the tutorial URL `https://plproxy.github.io/tutorial.html`, we have a code example like this:

```
CREATE OR REPLACE FUNCTION get_user_name(i_username text,  i_countrycode
text)
RETURNS SETOF text AS $$
CLUSTER 'usercluster';
```

```
RUN ON hashtext(i_countrycode);
SELECT name FROM customers WHERE name = i_username;
$$ LANGUAGE plproxy;
```

In this preceding example, the `RUN ON hashtext(i_countrycode)` code section calculates the partition, and diverts the following SQL statements to the corresponding node.

Finally, PL/Proxy distributes our actual table data into multiple databases. Each database will have some part of the complete table. Now you might have a question like, "How can I get the complete table data that is distributed among multiple databases?". For this, we need to have another function like the following one:

```
CREATE FUNCTION get_all_users(i_countrycode text)
RETURNS SETOF text AS $$
CLUSTER 'usercluster';
RUN ON hashtext(i_countrycode);
SELECT name FROM customers;
$$ LANGUAGE plproxy;
```

Now, to fetch the complete table data, we need to write multiple `UNION ALL` queries:

```
SELECT get_all_users('USA')
UNION ALL
SELECT get_all_users('IND')
....
....
UNION ALL
SELECT get_all_users('UK');
```

We need to adopt a function call API methodology to use PL/Proxy.

Foreign inheritance

Thanks to PostgreSQL 9.5, a new feature called foreign inheritance has been introduced. It uses SQL or **Manage External Data** (**MED**), using foreign data wrappers to achieve database scaling. Now let's see how it works.

This approach is similar to our local partitioning approach, which creates a master table and a set of child tables, makes them `INHERITS` with parent, and applies the trigger on the master table to navigate the `INSERT` operations to the child tables.

However, using foreign inheritance, we can have child tables in other databases too; we need to create a set of foreign tables on the parent database, which points to these remote tables.

1. Let's create multiple databases to hold different information about customers from different countries:

```
CREATE DATABASE customers_usa;
CREATE DATABASE customers_ind;
. .
CREATE DATABASE customers_uk;
```

2. Now, create a customers table in each database, and set up the parent table that points to these remote tables, as follows:

```
CREATE TABLE customers (id int, name varchar(126),
countrycode VARCHAR(3), contactnum text);
CREATE EXTENSION postgres_fdw;
CREATE SERVER shard_1 FOREIGN DATA WRAPPER postgres_fdw
OPTIONS( dbname 'customers_usa' );
...
CREATE USER MAPPING FOR POSTGRES SERVER shard_1 OPTIONS (
user 'postgres' );
...
CREATE FOREING TABLE customers_usa () INHERITS (customers)
SERVER shard_1 OPTIONS ( table_name 'customers' );
...
```

3. Now add the CHECK constraint on each foreign table to make constraint_exclusion effective.

```
ALTER foreign table customers_usa ADD CHECK(countrycode =
'USA');
...
```

4. Now apply the BEFORE INSERT trigger on the parent table:

```
CREATE OR REPLACE FUNCTION
public.customers_before_insert_trig_func()
RETURNS trigger AS
$$
BEGIN
EXECUTE 'INSERT INTO customers_'||NEW.countrycode||' VALUES
($1.*)' USING NEW;
RETURN NULL;
END
$$
```

```
LANGUAGE plpgsql;
CREATE TRIGGER customer_trig BEFORE INSERT on customers FOR
EACH ROW EXECUTE PROCEDURE
public.customers_before_insert_trig_func();
```

5. Execute a random `INSERT` SQL statement, and see the count.

```
EXPLAIN ANALYZE SELECT COUNT(*) FROM customers;
                    QUERY PLAN
-------------------------------------------------------------
Aggregate  (cost=1325.54..1325.55 rows=1 width=0)  (actual
time=7.616..7.616 rows=1 loops=1)
-> Append  (cost=0.00..1274.34 rows=20479 width=0)  (actual
time=0.846..7.151 rows=1992 loops=1)
-> Seq Scan on customers  (cost=0.00..0.00 rows=1 width=0)
(actual time=0.002..0.002 rows=0 loops=1)
-> Foreign Scan on customers_usa  (cost=100.00..212.39
rows=3413 width=0)  (actual time=0.843..1.321 rows=151
loops=1)
-> Foreign Scan on customers_uk  (cost=100.00..212.39
rows=3413 width=0)  (actual time=0.796..0.989 rows=180
loops=1)
-> Foreign Scan on customers_ind  (cost=100.00..212.39
rows=3413 width=0)  (actual time=0.559..0.741 rows=176
loops=1)
-> Foreign Scan on customers_rus  (cost=100.00..212.39
rows=3413 width=0)  (actual time=0.509..1.316 rows=495
loops=1)
-> Foreign Scan on customers_ger  (cost=100.00..212.39
rows=3413 width=0)  (actual time=0.725..1.539 rows=495
loops=1)
-> Foreign Scan on customers_uae  (cost=100.00..212.39
rows=3413 width=0)  (actual time=0.330..1.012 rows=495
loops=1)
Planning time: 0.346 ms
Execution time: 8.655 ms
(11 rows)
```

If you notice the preceding plan, you'll see that a bunch of foreign scans happen on each child table.

6. Let's try our actual ad hoc query, that is, getting the number of customers for specific countries, and see the plan again:

```
EXPLAIN ANALYZE SELECT COUNT(*), countrycode  FROM
customers WHERE countrycode IN ('USA', 'UK') GROUP BY
countrycode;
```

```
                          QUERY PLAN
--------------------------------------------------------------
HashAggregate  (cost=272.20..272.62 rows=41 width=16)
(actual time=2.357..2.358 rows=2 loops=1)
Group Key: customers.countrycode
-> Append  (cost=0.00..272.00 rows=41 width=16) (actual
time=1.015..2.152 rows=330 loops=1)
-> Seq Scan on customers  (cost=0.00..0.00 rows=1 width=16)
(actual time=0.002..0.002 rows=0 loops=1)
Filter: ((countrycode)::text = ANY ('{USA,UK}'::text[]))
-> Foreign Scan on customers_usa  (cost=100.00..136.00
rows=20 width=16) (actual time=1.011..1.232 rows=150
loops=1)
-> Foreign Scan on customers_uk  (cost=100.00..136.00
rows=20 width=16) (actual time=0.597..0.870 rows=180
loops=1)
Planning time: 0.664 ms
Execution time: 3.203 ms
(9 rows)
```

We can also experiment with DELETE/UPDATE, which works the same way as with local partitioning.

To summarize, foreign inheritance really scales our databases into multiple instances where we can get the best performance by utilizing multiple servers. It is really more useful than Pl/Proxy, since we do not need to adopt the function call API.

Summary

In this chapter, we discussed table partitioning with some good use cases. We covered topics like, "When do you need partitioning?", and "How does that help with your data?" Simply partitioning a large table might not help sometimes, so be careful while choosing the table to be partitioned and, most importantly, the type of partition that would really help with your data. You should also choose the column on which you might want to create a partition carefully. We also discussed ways to manage (alter/drop) the partitions once they are created. There are some alternate methods for partitioning if you do not want to go for the traditional ones. Hope it helps you to choose a better partitioning method for your data and better control over managing it. In the next chapter, we will talk about fine tuning your queries and optimizing them. We will cover query rewrites; however, you may not have to rewrite every time. So we will also discuss when to rewrite a query, and when not to.

8
Query Tuning and Optimization

In the last chapter, we talked about table partitioning. We introduced table partitioning, how to choose which table needs it, how to benefit from it, how to optimize it, how to tell the system to make use of it, and what the alternative options are if you do not want to go for the traditional procedures. In this chapter, we are going to cover how a query gets executed, ways to tune queries, generating explain plans, and each and every plan node. It also covers tuning a query, dealing with caches, extensions available for caching/warming the data, Optimizer settings to cache data, and how to use Optimizer hints.

Query tuning

Before discussing query tuning, first we should know how to write a query, and then we can tune it later on. Queries can be written in multiple ways, as per the requirement; however, we have to prefer an optimal way to write queries.

For example, say that your requirement is to get the row count from a static table. You can achieve this through the following three methods:

Method 1:

```
postgres=# SELECT SUM(1) FROM customers;
sum
------
1000
(1 row)
Time: 4.308 ms
```

Method 2:

```
postgres=# SELECT COUNT(*) FROM customers;
count
--------
1000
(1 row)
Time: 3.128 ms
```

Method 3:

```
postgres=# SELECT reltuples FROM pg_class WHERE relname =  'customers';
reltuples
-----------
1000
(1 row)
Time: 0.576 ms
```

From the preceding three possible methods, we see that *Method 3* gives the best result, and *Method 2* is optimal when compared to *Method 1*. *Method 1* takes a bit more time, when compared with *Method 2*, since it needs to SUM all the records at once, whereas the COUNT aggregate follows a different approach.

Hot versus cold cache

Hot or cold cache plays another vital role in query performance. When a query hits a database for the first time, it looks for the required data blocks in PostgreSQL's shared_buffers, and then it looks for the buffers in the OS cache. If the data blocks are not found in shared_buffers and OS cache, then postgres fetches its required data blocks from the disk to shared_buffers for further processing. This is the code cache behavior. If the data blocks are found in the buffers/cache, then this is hot cache behavior. The more hot cache we get in the execution plan, the more performance we get as a benefit.

Now, the question is how to pin the table's required blocks in either shared_buffers or OS cache. As an answer to this question, we have two extensions available in postgres. Let's discuss those extensions, which are the following:

- pg_buffercache deals with shared_buffers
- pg_prewarm deals with shared_buffers and OS cache

Before going into these extensions, let's see how cache impacts our query execution.

Cleaning the cache

In PostgreSQL, we do not have an easy way to clear the cache properly. To clean the cache, we have to take the `postgres` instance down, and we also have to clear the OS cache.

A `postgres` instance is taken down as follows:

```
~$ service postgresql-9.5 stop
Stopping PostgreSQL 9.5:
Password:
waiting for server to shut down.... done
server stopped
```

There might be some dirty blocks in the operating system cache, that need a `sync` to the physical data files. You can use the following command to force the dirty blocks in the cache to the disk:

```
$ sudo sync
```

To check the cache size, before cleaning, use the following command:

```
$ free -m
total     used      free      shared    buffers     cached
Mem:      3953      2667      1285      8           104         1719
-/+ buffers/cache: 843       3109
Swap:     4113      0         4113
```

Clean the OS cache with this command:

```
# echo 3 > /proc/sys/vm/drop_caches
```

Now check the cache size after cleaning:

```
$ free -m
total     used      free      shared    buffers     cached
Mem:      3953      990       2962      8           7           221
-/+ buffers/cache:      761       3191
Swap:           4113      0         4113
```

Now we've cleared the OS cache and `shared_buffers` too. Let's start the `postgres` instance, and run the query:

```
$ service postgresql-9.5 start
Starting PostgreSQL 9.5:
waiting for server to start.... done
server started
PostgreSQL 9.5 started successfully
postgres=# SELECT COUNT(*) FROM customers;
```

```
count
--------
512000
(1 row)
Time: 291.190 ms
```

Also, let's see the number of I/O reads that happened during this non-cache behavior:

```
DEV  tps rd_sec/s wr_sec/s avgrq-sz  avgqu-sz await svctm    %util
dev8-0   209.00 52208.00   16.00 249.88   0.04  0.21  0.21    4.40
```

Now let's put the `customers` table into the OS cache, and then see the response time. To get the actual table file location which is on disk, you can use the following command:

```
postgres=# SELECT pg_relation_filepath('customers'::regclass);
pg_relation_filepath
---------------------
base/215681/215878
(1 row)
```

Use the `dd` command to read the content of a table's file so that the OS can automatically cache it.

```
$ dd if=data/base/215681/215878 of=/dev/null bs=8096
postgres=# SELECT COUNT(*) FROM customers;
count
--------
512000
(1 row)
Time: 150.520 ms
```

The following is the output of the `sar -d` command in the query execution:

```
DEV  tps rd_sec/s wr_sec/s avgrq-sz  avgqu-sz await svctm    %util
dev8-0 43.00 3392.00 0.00   78.88    0.01   0.19   0.19    0.80
```

It seems we got 50% performance as a benefit when we cached the table at the OS level. Now, let's try to put the table in `shared_buffers`, instead of the OS cache; using `pg_prewarm`. `pg_prewarm` is an extension for caching the table at the OS level or in `shared_buffers`. To install this, execute `CREATE EXTENSION pg_prewarm` as a superuser in the database.

Now let's put the customers table data into `shared_buffers` using the `pg_prewarm` function.

```
postgres=# SELECT pg_prewarm('customers'::regclass);
pg_prewarm
-------------
3262
(1 row)
```

In the preceding results, you can see that `pg_prewarm` holds `3262` block sizes of the table `customers`. Now let's check whether our query goes to hot cache or cold cache from the execution plan. With the EXPLAIN command, we can use an option called BUFFERS, which gives information about the cache involvement.

```
postgres=# EXPLAIN (ANALYZE,BUFFERS) SELECT COUNT(*) FROM  customers;
                    QUERY PLAN
---------------------------------------------------------------
Aggregate  (cost=9662.00..9662.01 rows=1 width=0) (actual
time=155.336..155.336 rows=1 loops=1)
Buffers: shared hit=3262
-> Seq Scan on customers  (cost=0.00..8382.00 rows=512000  width=0)
(actual time=0.012..85.316 rows=512000 loops=1)
Buffers: shared hit=3262
Planning time: 0.055 ms
Execution time: 155.428 ms
(6 rows)
```

In the last plan, we can see that the value of `Buffers` is given as `shared hit=3262`. It clearly shows that the query has taken its dataset from `shared_buffers`.

Let's see what other information we can get from BUFFERS by using some other operations.

```
postgres=# EXPLAIN (ANALYZE, BUFFERS) UPDATE customers SET name='A';
                    QUERY PLAN
---------------------------------------------------------------
Update on customers  (cost=0.00..18164.00 rows=512000 width=23)  (actual
time=3125.833..3125.833 rows=0 loops=1)
Buffers: shared hit=1043435 read=3260 dirtied=3259 written=6
-> Seq Scan on customers  (cost=0.00..18164.00 rows=512000  width=23)
(actual time=7.348..471.141 rows=512000 loops=1)
Buffers: shared hit=13044
Planning time: 0.079 ms
Execution time: 3125.878 ms
(6 rows)
```

In the preceding plan, we see the `shared hit=1043435 read=3260 dirtied=3259 written=6` information about the BUFFERS option. From this line, we can clearly make out the following:

- The query got `1043435` cache hits
- It read `3260` as I/O operations
- This query dirtied 3,259 existing `shared_buffers` blocks
- This query caused the eviction of four dirtied blocks from `shared_buffers`

Like the BUFFERS option, we have some other options too. I would encourage you to read all of these at this URL:

`http://www.postgresql.org/docs/current/static/sql-explain.html`.

pg_buffercache

Let's discuss the extensions that we have used in our previous examples. `pg_buffercache` is the one we used to identify the `shared_buffers` usage of our SQL statements.

`pg_buffercache` gives `shared_buffers` current usage of the `postgresql` instance. Using this extension, we can identify whether our `shared_buffers` setting is enough for the `postgres` instance or not.

To install this component, we have to run the CREATE EXTENSION `pg_buffercache` statement. Once we install this component, we will get `pg_buffercache` view, which gives the following information from the active `shared_buffers`:

```
Column             | Description
-------------------+----------------
bufferid           | Buffer ID
relfilenode        | Relation file node
reltablespace      | Relation table space
reldatabase        | Relation database
relforknumber      | Relation fork physical file number.
relblocknumber     | Relation physical block number
isdirty            | Is buffer modified with any DML
usagecount         | Clock sweep count to evict the buffer from
                     shared_buffers
pinning_backends   | Number of backends currently pinned with this
                     buffer
```

Let's look at a sample set of records for a huge table:

```
postgres=# SELECT * FROM pg_buffercache WHERE relfilenode = 17557;
-[ RECORD 1 ]----+------
bufferid          | 1310
relfilenode       | 17557
reltablespace     | 1663
reldatabase       | 12641
relforknumber     | 1
relblocknumber    | 0
isdirty           | f
usagecount        | 4
pinning_backends  | 0
```

Now, let's see how much space the relation `17557` occupies in our `shared_buffers`.

```
postgres=# SELECT COUNT(*)*4096/(2048)||' MB' used FROM  pg_buffercache
WHERE relfilenode = 17557;
used
-------
66 MB
(1 row)
```

In the preceding calculation, `4096` is the page size of the physical memory, and our big table occupies 66 MB of `shared_buffers` out of the 128 MB default setting. Let's see what all tables occupy our `shared_buffers`:

```
postgres=# SELECT COUNT(*)*4096/(2<<10)||' MB' used,relname FROM
pg_buffercache b,pg_class c WHERE b.relfilenode=c.relfilenode  GROUP BY 2
LIMIT 5;
    used  |    relname
    ------+------------
    8 MB  | pg_amop
    66 MB | test
    4 MB  | pg_index_indexrelid_index
    2 MB  | pg_cast
    4 MB  | pg_aggregate_fnoid_index
    (5 rows)
```

Now let's see how many dirty buffers we have in `shared_buffers` that need to be flushed during the CHECKPOINT process:

```
postgres=# SELECT Round(COUNT(*)*4096/2048.0,2)||' MB'  used,relname FROM
pg_buffercache b,pg_class c WHERE  b.relfilenode=c.relfilenode AND
isdirty=true GROUP BY 2;
           used   |    relname
    ----------+----------------
      90.00 MB | test
```

```
      2.00 MB  | pg_statistic
      (2 rows)
```

Now use the manual CHECKPOINT, and see the dirty buffers:

```
postgres=# CHECKPOINT;
CHECKPOINT
postgres=# SELECT Round(COUNT(*)*4096/2048.0,2)||' Used,relname  FROM
pg_buffercache b,pg_class c WHERE b.relfilenode=c.relfilenode  AND
isdirty=true GROUP BY 2;
        used | relname
      -----+---------
      (0 rows)
```

pg_prewarm

Using this as an extension, we can load our relations data into either the OS cache or shared_buffers. The pg_prewarm extension provides three modes to load the dataset into the cache:

- .PREFETCH: Fetches data blocks asynchronously to the OS cache
- .READ: Fetches data blocks synchronously to the OS cache
- .BUFFER: Fetches data blocks synchronously to shared_buffers

Now we have to use a pg_prewarm method to initiate the cache load, and the following is the declaration:

```
pg_prewarm(regclass, mode text DEFAULT 'buffer'::text, fork text   DEFAULT
'main'::text, first_block bigint DEFAULT NULL::bigint,  last_block bigint
DEFAULT NULL::bigint)
```

In the preceding declaration, we have to give the relation name followed by its cache load method and fork as well the block boundaries.

- The fork argument allows additional fsm and vm options, which load the table's free space map and the visibility map information into the cache
- The first_block argument takes the first block number of a relation
- The last_block argument takes the last block number of a relation

For example, consider the following SQL statement:

```
postgres=# SELECT pg_prewarm('customers', 'buffer', 'main', 0,  1000);
pg_prewarm
------------
```

```
1001
(1 row)
```

In the preceding statement, we load the customers table's blocks from 0 to `1000` into `shared_buffers`, and `pg_prewarm` returns the number of blocks it copied to the buffers.

Now let's query the `pg_buffercache` view, and see how many buffers the customers table occupies in `shared_buffers`.

```
postgres=# SELECT COUNT(*) FROM pg_buffercache WHERE relfilenode =  17972;
count
-------
1001
(1 row)
```

In `pg_buffercache`, we are able to see those `1001` number of blocks occupied in `shared_buffers`.

Let's try to execute a full-table scan on the table, and see how many cache hits we got from the plan:

```
postgres=# EXPLAIN (BUFFERS, ANALYZE) SELECT * FROM customers;
                        QUERY PLAN
-----------------------------------------------------------------
Seq Scan on customers  (cost=0.00..8382.00 rows=512000 width=19)   (actual
time=0.013..213.986 rows=512000 loops=1)
Buffers: shared hit=1001 read=2261
Planning time: 87.812 ms
Execution time: 267.280 ms
(4 rows)
```

From the preceding plan, we can see that `shared hit=1001` matches with the number of blocks we cached into `shared_buffers` using `pg_prewarm`.

Optimizer settings for cached data

In PostgreSQL, by default, some configuration settings are configured to deal with disk I/O; that is, cost related to perform a sequential and random disk scans.

The following are the default values for these parameters:

```
postgres=# SHOW seq_page_cost ;
seq_page_cost
---------------
1
```

To perform a single tuple fetch from the disk, the required cost is 1.

```
postgres=# SHOW random_page_cost ;
random_page_cost
--------------------
4
```

To perform a single tuple fetch by referring its index, the required cost is 4.

If all our table's data or the complete database fits in the existing RAM size, then we can lower these values to as minimum as possible, since we don't need to perform any disk I/O operations.

Let's see the plan before setting these parameters, and then we will see the plan cost after lowering them.

Set the parameters with default settings as follows:

```
postgres=# SET random_page_cost to default ;
SET
postgres=# SET seq_page_cost to default ;
SET
postgres=# EXPLAIN (ANALYZE, BUFFERS) SELECT COUNT(*) FROM  customers GROUP
BY countrycode;
                            QUERY PLAN
-----------------------------------------------------------------
->  Seq Scan on customers   (cost=0.00..8382.00 rows=512000  width=3)
(actual time=0.016..85.586 rows=512000 loops=1)
Buffers: shared hit=3262
```

In the preceding plan, at the Seq Scan node, the cost begins at 0.00 and ends at 8382.00.

Now we will lower these parameters as follows:

```
postgres=# SET seq_page_cost to 0.005;
SET
postgres=# SET random_page_cost to 0.005;
SET
postgres=# EXPLAIN (ANALYZE, BUFFERS) SELECT COUNT(*) FROM  customers GROUP
BY countrycode;
                            QUERY PLAN
-----------------------------------------------------------------
->  Seq Scan on customers   (cost=0.00..5136.31 rows=512000  width=3)
(actual time=0.017..88.598 rows=512000 loops=1)
Buffers: shared hit=3262
```

We can see that the plan cost for the node `Seq Scan` is reduced in the preceding plan.

If we know that all our datasets are in the cache, then there is no need to set these two parameter values to deal with the disk I/O. We can set these either at session level or in the `postgresql.conf` file if we want to implement these changes at the cluster level.

Multiple ways to implement a query

As we all know, a query can be implemented in several ways. But only one will be implemented among them:the one that takes the least cost when compared to the rest. For demonstration purposes, let's consider we have a payments table, which makes customer id entry along with the payment date when the customer clears his payment.

Now the general request from the management team is something like, "Get me the customers who've paid so far".

For this requirement, we can write queries like the following:

- **Approach 1**: Joining tables

```
CREATE TABLE payments (id integer, amount numeric, paydate  date);
postgres=# EXPLAIN ANALYZE SELECT c.id FROM customers C,
payments P WHERE
c.id=p.id AND p.paydate<=now()::date;
                    QUERY PLAN
----------------------------------------------------------------
Hash Join  (cost=16236.00..36268.00 rows=412000 width=4)  (actual
time=595.027..1362.015 rows=412000 loops=1)
Hash Cond: (c.id = p.id)
-> Seq Scan on customers c  (cost=0.00..8382.00
rows=512000  width=4)
(actual time=0.017..151.269 rows=512000 loops=1)
-> Hash  (cost=9476.00..9476.00 rows=412000 width=4) (actual
time=516.760..516.760 rows=412000 loops=1)
Buckets: 131072  Batches: 8  Memory Usage: 2833kB
-> Seq Scan on payments p  (cost=0.00..9476.00
rows=412000  width=4)
(actual time=0.968..323.335 rows=412000 loops=1)
Filter: (paydate <= (now())::date)
Planning time: 0.194 ms
Execution time: 1388.577 ms
(9 rows)
```

- **Approach 2**: Correlation

```
postgres=# EXPLAIN ANALYZE SELECT c.id FROM customers C WHERE
EXISTS(SELECT 1 FROM payments P WHERE C.ID=P.ID AND
p.paydate<=now()::date);
                           QUERY PLAN
----------------------------------------------------------------
Hash Semi Join  (cost=16236.00..36155.50 rows=412000 width=4)
(actual time=612.459..1341.980 rows=412000 loops=1)
Hash Cond: (c.id = p.id)
-> Seq Scan on customers c  (cost=0.00..8382.00
rows=512000  width=4)
(actual time=0.017..148.489 rows=512000 loops=1)
-> Hash  (cost=9476.00..9476.00 rows=412000 width=4)  (actual
time=536.628..536.628 rows=412000 loops=1)
Buckets: 131072  Batches: 8  Memory Usage: 2833kB
-> Seq Scan on payments p  (cost=0.00..9476.00
rows=412000  width=4)
(actual time=0.948..331.856 rows=412000 loops=1)
Filter: (paydate <= (now())::date)
Planning time: 0.232 ms
Execution time: 1366.066 ms
(9 rows)
```

- **Approach 3**: Set operations

```
postgres=# EXPLAIN ANALYZE (SELECT id FROM customers C
INTERSECT
SELECT id FROM payments P WHERE P.paydate<=now()::date
);
                           QUERY PLAN
----------------------------------------------------------------
SetOp Intersect  (cost=131290.00..135910.00 rows=412000  width=4)
(actual time=1988.390..2914.015 rows=412000 loops=1)
-> Sort  (cost=131290.00..133600.00 rows=924000 width=4)  (actual
time=1988.382..2592.499 rows=924000 loops=1)
Sort Key: "*SELECT* 2".id
Sort Method: external merge  Disk: 16192kB
-> Append  (cost=0.00..27098.00 rows=924000 width=4)  (actual
time=3.134..861.385 rows=924000 loops=1)
-> Subquery Scan on "*SELECT* 2"  (cost=0.00..13596.00  rows=412000
width=4) (actual time=3.133..448.099 rows=412000  loops=1)
-> Seq Scan on payments p  (cost=0.00..9476.00
rows=412000  width=4)
(actual time=3.129..329.192 rows=412000 loops=1)
Filter: (paydate <= (now())::date)
-> Subquery Scan on "*SELECT* 1"  (cost=0.00..13502.00  rows=512000
width=4) (actual time=0.009..289.876 rows=512000  loops=1)
-> Seq Scan on customers c  (cost=0.00..8382.00
rows=512000  width=4)
```

```
(actual time=0.008..144.930 rows=512000 loops=1)
Planning time: 0.153 ms
Execution time: 3071.810 ms
(12 rows)
```

If we observe the actual time from the top nodes in the preceding three approaches, all give us the same number of rows. However, for this existing amount of data, approach 2 gave us a better performance when compared with the rest.

Approach 3 is not a good way to implement this kind of requests, since set operations like INTERSECT have an additional sorting overhead.

So, from this preceding demonstration, we can conclude that, although we can write SQL queries in multiple ways, we have to choose the best one, that is, the one that costs less than the rest.

Bad query performance with stale statistics

Query performance always depends on the plan chosen by the Optimizer. Optimizer again depends on the statistics of corresponding relations to generate a plan for the query. If Postgres has stale statistics, the query might get bad plans irrespective of the existing datasets.

For example, consider we have the following two test tables on which we perform basic operations like the following:

```
CREATE TABLE out(t INTEGER);
CREATE TABLE inn(t INTEGER);
postgres=# SELECT COUNT(*) FROM out;
count
-------
1000
(1 row)
postgres=# SELECT COUNT(*) FROM inn;
count
-------
1000
(1 row)
postgres=# EXPLAIN ANALYZE SELECT * FROM out WHERE t IN(SELECT t  FROM
inn);
                            QUERY PLAN
----------------------------------------------------------------------
Hash Semi Join  (cost=27.50..56.25 rows=1000 width=4) (actual
time=1.201..3.646 rows=1000 loops=1)
Hash Cond: ("out".t = inn.t)
```

```
-> Seq Scan on "out"  (cost=0.00..15.00 rows=1000 width=4)  (actual
time=0.015..0.716 rows=1000 loops=1)
-> Hash  (cost=15.00..15.00 rows=1000 width=4) (actual  time=1.167..1.167
rows=1000 loops=1)
Buckets: 1024  Batches: 1  Memory Usage: 44kB
-> Seq Scan on inn  (cost=0.00..15.00 rows=1000 width=4)  (actual
time=0.012..0.342 rows=1000 loops=1)
Planning time: 0.254 ms
Execution time: 3.789 ms
(8 rows)
```

This preceding plan seems fair, and PostgreSQL has chosen the best plan based on the statistics available. Now, for demonstration purposes, I am going to keep only one row in the out table by deleting the rest, and then we will see the plan for the same query.

```
postgres=# SELECT COUNT(*) FROM out;
count
-------
1
(1 row)
postgres=# EXPLAIN ANALYZE SELECT * FROM out WHERE t IN(SELECT t  FROM
inn);
                          QUERY PLAN
-----------------------------------------------------------------
Hash Semi Join  (cost=27.50..56.25 rows=1000 width=4) (actual
time=3.021..3.022 rows=1 loops=1)
Hash Cond: ("out".t = inn.t)
-> Seq Scan on "out"  (cost=0.00..15.00 rows=1000 width=4)  (actual
time=0.025..0.026 rows=1 loops=1)
-> Hash  (cost=15.00..15.00 rows=1000 width=4) (actual  time=2.967..2.967
rows=1000 loops=1)
Buckets: 1024  Batches: 1  Memory Usage: 44kB
-> Seq Scan on inn  (cost=0.00..15.00 rows=1000 width=4)  (actual
time=0.012..1.478 rows=1000 loops=1)
 Planning time: 0.207 ms
 Execution time: 3.094 ms
 (8 rows)
```

If we look at the node Seq Scan on out in this last plan, the Optimizer still considers the out table to have 1000 rows in it. However, it now has only 1 row.

There can be several reasons, including the following, as to why the table statistics are not updated:

- Lazy autovacuum settings
- The stats collector process is not able to update the stats due to a huge I/O load
- No job is scheduled to run ANALYZE database manually

- Invalid `default_statistics_target` setting, and so on

However, in real use cases, consider if the preceding query runs 5,000 to 10,000 times per minute. This will drastically increase the load on the db server, since it chose hash join, which uses `44kB` for query execution, and this may also cause a load spike on dashboards.

If we run the same query after a couple of minutes, we get the following plan as per the current dataset, which is optimal:

```
postgres=# EXPLAIN ANALYZE SELECT * FROM out WHERE t IN(SELECT t  FROM
inn);
                          QUERY PLAN
--------------------------------------------------------------------
Nested Loop Semi Join  (cost=0.00..32.51 rows=1 width=4) (actual
time=0.532..0.533 rows=1 loops=1)
Join Filter: ("out".t = inn.t)
Rows Removed by Join Filter: 999
-> Seq Scan on "out"  (cost=0.00..5.01 rows=1 width=4) (actual
time=0.042..0.043 rows=1 loops=1)
-> Seq Scan on inn  (cost=0.00..15.00 rows=1000 width=4) (actual
time=0.019..0.217 rows=1000 loops=1)
Planning time: 2.097 ms
Execution time: 0.681 ms
(7 rows)
```

So, in our case, we depend on the autovacuum daemon to update the statistics. Once we get the updated statistics, the Optimizer produces better plans.

It is always good to keep our database statistics as up-to-date as possible, since db stats gives a better estimation to the Optimizer in order to generate the best plan for query execution.

Optimizer hints

In PostgreSQL, we do not have any direct Optimizer hints syntax which can divert the Optimizer to choose the required plan. However, we can simulate hints behavior by turning off the query tuning settings at the session level.

Let's see in which cases we need to enable/disable these tuning parameters. Consider our `out` and `inn` tables' basic query operation.

In our previous demonstration, `EXPLAIN ANALYZE` gave us the proper `Nested Loop` join after a couple of minutes. That was due to lazy autovacuum settings. Let's assume that this is not a problem with autovacuum settings.

If we keep on getting the same hash join plan for the single row table, then it always uses unnecessary memory for the hash buckets. To deal with this case, let's disable the enable_hashjoin Optimizer, and see the plan for the same query.

```
postgres=# set enable_hashjoin to off;
SET
postgres=# EXPLAIN ANALYZE SELECT * FROM out WHERE t IN(SELECT t  FROM
inn);
                            QUERY PLAN
---------------------------------------------------------------------
Merge Semi Join  (cost=129.66..149.66 rows=1000 width=4) (actual
time=3.082..3.083 rows=1 loops=1)
Merge Cond: ("out".t = inn.t)
-> Sort  (cost=64.83..67.33 rows=1000 width=4) (actual  time=0.046..0.047
rows=1 loops=1)
Sort Key: "out".t
Sort Method: quicksort  Memory: 25kB
-> Seq Scan on "out"  (cost=0.00..15.00 rows=1000 width=4)   (actual
time=0.025..0.026 rows=1 loops=1)
-> Sort  (cost=64.83..67.33 rows=1000 width=4) (actual  time=0.516..0.901
rows=1000 loops=1)
Sort Key: inn.t
Sort Method: quicksort  Memory: 71kB
-> Seq Scan on inn  (cost=0.00..15.00 rows=1000 width=4) (actual
time=0.011..0.231 rows=1000 loops=1)
 Planning time: 0.185 ms
 Execution time: 3.171 ms
 (12 rows)
```

The preceding plan is also not an optimum one since it will merge join, which requires additional sort operations on both the tables. In the last plan, we see that the query execution uses 25kB and 71kB memory for sorting purposes.

Now, let's try to disable this Optimizer setting too, and see the plan one more time:

```
postgres=# set enable_mergejoin to off;
SET
postgres=# EXPLAIN ANALYZE SELECT * FROM out WHERE t IN(SELECT t  FROM
inn);
                            QUERY PLAN
---------------------------------------------------------------------
Nested Loop Semi Join  (cost=0.00..15032.50 rows=1000 width=4)  (actual
time=1.963..1.964 rows=1 loops=1)
Join Filter: ("out".t = inn.t)
Rows Removed by Join Filter: 999
-> Seq Scan on "out"  (cost=0.00..15.00 rows=1000 width=4)   (actual
time=0.027..0.028 rows=1 loops=1)
```

```
-> Materialize  (cost=0.00..20.00 rows=1000 width=4) (actual
time=0.015..1.646 rows=1000 loops=1)
-> Seq Scan on inn  (cost=0.00..15.00 rows=1000 width=4) (actual
time=0.012..0.660 rows=1000 loops=1)
Planning time: 0.148 ms
Execution time: 2.058 ms
(8 rows)
```

Yes, this last plan is what we are looking for. Once we disabled `enable_hashjoin` and `enable_mergejoin`, we got the desired and optimal plan. I am not saying that the `Nested Loop` join is the best of the rest. The Optimizer chooses these methods based on the volume of the dataset which it is going to operate on. The `Nested Loop` method always gives the best results on a reduced volume of data, whereas the `Hash Join` method gives better results on a moderate volume of data. The `Merge Join` method is best for a high volume of data. So, based on the volume of data, the Optimizer chooses the right method. However, the Optimizer depends on the statistics, which we need to make sure are up-to-date, to pick up the right approach to deal with the data volume.

Using the following list of Optimizer settings, we can divert the query plan:

```
postgres=# SELECT name FROM pg_settings WHERE name ~ 'enable_';
     name
-----------------
enable_bitmapscan
enable_hashagg
enable_hashjoin
enable_indexonlyscan
enable_indexscan
enable_material
enable_mergejoin
enable_nestloop
enable_seqscan
enable_sort
enable_tidscan
(11 rows)
```

In some other cases, we may also need to update the column-level statistics in a table to achieve a better plan. These are the special cases where we are directly dealing with the Optimizer's source.

For demonstration, consider we have a plain table on which we perform the GROUP BY operation:

```
CREATE TABLE groupbytest(t integer);
postgres=# SELECT COUNT(*) FROM groupbytest;
count
```

```
100000
(1 row)
postgres=# EXPLAIN ANALYZE SELECT COUNT(*) FROM groupbytest GROUP  BY t;
                              QUERY PLAN
-----------------------------------------------------------------------
GroupAggregate (cost=9747.82..11497.82 rows=100000 width=4)    (actual
time=140.870..237.985 rows=100000 loops=1)
Group Key: t
-> Sort   (cost=9747.82..9997.82 rows=100000 width=4) (actual
time=140.859..169.622 rows=100000 loops=1)
Sort Key: t
Sort Method: external sort   Disk: 1368kB
-> Seq Scan on groupbytest   (cost=0.00..1443.00 rows=100000  width=4)
(actual time=0.020..19.065 rows=100000 loops=1)
Planning time: 0.099 ms
Execution time: 253.300 ms
(8 rows)
```

From the preceding plan, it seems the Optimizer has chosen the plan to do
GroupAggregate for the GROUP BY operation. In PostgreSQL, we also have
HashAggregate, which eliminates the Sort operation required by the GroupAggregate
method.

Now let's see the value of enable_hashagg, and let's enable it if it's not:

```
postgres=# SHOW enable_hashagg;
enable_hashagg
----------------
on
(1 row)
```

It seems enable_hashagg is ON even though the Optimizer has chosen the
GroupAggregate method. To impose the HashAggregate method for the GROUP BY, we
have to understand the n_distinct column in the pg_stats table.

```
postgres=# SELECT n_distinct FROM pg_stats WHERE tablename =  'groupbytest'
AND attname = 't';
n_distinct
-------------
-1
(1 row)
```

We see that the value of n_distinct is −1 for the column t of the relation groupbytest.
That means all the field values of an attribute t are unique values, and there are no repeated
values in it.

Now, let's try to impose the `n_distinct` value to a minimum value in the following code snippet, and see the plan of the query:

```
postgres=# ALTER TABLE groupbytest ALTER COLUMN t SET(N_DISTINCT =  2);
ALTER TABLE
```

The preceding query is saying that column `t` of the relation `groupbytest` will have only two distinct values. That means all the rows in `groupbytest` will have repeated values.

```
postgres=# ANALYZE groupbytest;
ANALYZE
postgres=# EXPLAIN ANALYZE SELECT COUNT(*) FROM groupbytest GROUP  BY t;
                  QUERY PLAN
------------------------------------------------------------------
HashAggregate  (cost=1943.00..1943.02 rows=2 width=4) (actual
time=105.622..160.667 rows=100000 loops=1)
Group Key: t
-> Seq Scan on groupbytest  (cost=0.00..1443.00 rows=100000  width=4)
(actual time=0.016..19.497 rows=100000 loops=1)
Planning time: 0.120 ms
Execution time: 174.094 ms
(5 rows)
```

Now, if you examine the above plan for the same query, it took the `HashAggregate` method, since we diverted the Optimizer to go with a different plan as per the `n_distinct` setting. If we have `n_distinct` value as a minimum; then the Optimizer will always try to do `HashAggregate` for the `GROUP BY` operation.

Now you might get a question like, tweaking the `n_distinct` setting works for the above query but it may not work effectively for the remaining queries. Also, it is not a good practice to change these settings in real production servers. To avoid the `Sort` operation with `GroupAggregate` on column `t`, we have to create a sorted index, which will perform an index scan on the same column rather than the sorting operation.

```
postgres=# CREATE INDEX sortidx ON groupbytest (t ASC);
CREATE INDEX
postgres=# EXPLAIN ANALYZE SELECT COUNT(*) FROM groupbytest GROUP  BY t;
                  QUERY PLAN
------------------------------------------------------------------
GroupAggregate  (cost=0.29..4550.29 rows=100000 width=4) (actual
time=0.082..137.405 rows=100000 loops=1)
Group Key: t
-> Index Only Scan using sortidx on groupbytest  (cost=0.29..3050.29
rows=100000 width=4) (actual  time=0.072..52.599 rows=100000 loops=1)
Heap Fetches: 100000
Planning time: 0.303 ms
```

```
Execution time: 148.135 ms
(6 rows)
```

Explain Plan

Postgres has a great ability to show you how it will actually execute a query under the covers. This is known as an execution plan, and it is exposed by the explain command. Understanding this tells you how you can optimize your database with indexes to improve performance.

Every query within Postgres has an execution plan when executed. There are three ways to run explain to expose this to you:

- The generic form (only shows what is likely to happen)
- The Analyze form (which actually runs the query, and outputs what does happen)
- The Verbose form (verbose information)

Most commonly, explain is run on the SELECT statements. However, you can also use it on the following:

- INSERT
- UPDATE
- DELETE
- EXECUTE
- DECLARE

Generating and reading the Explain Plan

For each step in the execution plan, EXPLAIN prints the following information:

- The type of operation required.
- The estimated cost of execution.
- If you specified EXPLAIN ANALYZE, it gives the actual cost of execution. If you omit the ANALYZE keyword, the query is planned but not executed, and the actual cost is not displayed.

Simple example

Let's start by looking at a simple example:

```
perf=# EXPLAIN ANALYZE SELECT * FROM recalls;
                QUERY PLAN:
Seq Scan on recalls  (cost=0.00..9217.41 rows=39241  width=1917)(actual
time=69.35..3052.72 rows=39241 loops=1)
Total runtime: 3144.61 msec
```

In this preceding example, PostgreSQL has decided to perform a sequential scan of the recalls table (Seq Scan on recalls). There are three data items in the cost estimate:

- The first set of numbers (cost=0.00..9217.41) is an estimate of how expensive this operation will be. Expensive is measured in terms of disk reads. Two numbers are given:
  - The first number represents how quickly the first row in the result set can be returned by the operation.
  - The second (which is usually the most important) represents how long the entire operation should take. The second data item in the cost estimate (rows=39241) shows how many rows PostgreSQL expects to return from this operation.
- The final data item (width=1917) is an estimate of the width, in bytes, of the average row in the result set.
- If you include the ANALYZE keyword in the EXPLAIN command, PostgreSQL will execute the query, and display the actual execution costs. This was a simple example. PostgreSQL required only one step to execute this query (a sequential scan on the entire table). Many queries require multiple steps, and the EXPLAIN command will show you each of those steps.

More complex example

Let's now move on to a more complex example:

```
perf=# EXPLAIN ANALYZE SELECT * FROM recalls ORDER BY yeartxt;
NOTICE:   QUERY PLAN:
Sort (cost=145321.51..145321.51 rows=39241 width=1911)
(actual time=13014.92..13663.86 rows=39241 loops=1)
-> Seq Scan on recalls (cost=0.00..9217.41 rows=39241 width=1917)   (actual
time=68.99..3446.74 rows=39241 loops=1)
Total runtime: 16052.53 msec
```

This last example shows a two-step query plan. In this case, the first step is actually listed at the end of the plan. When you read a query plan, it is important to remember that each step in the plan produces an intermediate result set. Each intermediate result set is fed into the next step of the plan.

- Looking at this plan, PostgreSQL first produces an intermediate result set by performing a sequential scan (Seq Scan) on the entire recalls table. That step should take about 9,217 disk page reads, and the result set will have about 39,241 rows, averaging 1,917 bytes each. Notice that these estimates are identical to those produced in the first example. And in both cases, you are executing a sequential scan on the entire table.
- After the sequential scan has finished building its intermediate result set, it is fed into the next step in the plan. The final step in this particular plan is a sort operation, which is required to satisfy our ORDER BY clause. The sort operation reorders the result set produced by the sequential scan, and returns the final result set to the client application.
- An ORDER BY clause does not require a sort operation in all cases. The Planner/Optimizer may decide that it can use an index to order the result set.

Query operators

PostgreSQL currently has 19 query operators.

Seq Scan

The Seq Scan operator is the most basic query operator. Any single-table query can be carried out using the Seq Scan operator.

Index Scan

An Index Scan operator works by traversing an index structure. If you specify a starting value for an indexed column (WHERE record_id >= 1000, for example), the Index Scan will begin at the appropriate value. If you specify an ending value (such as WHERE record_id < 2000), the Index Scan will complete as soon as it finds an index entry greater than the ending value.

Sort

The `Sort` operator imposes an ordering on the result set. PostgreSQL uses two different sort strategies: an in-memory sort and an on-disk sort. You can tune a PostgreSQL instance by adjusting the value of the `work_mem` runtime parameter.

Unique

The `UNIQUE` operator eliminates duplicate values from the input set. The input set must be ordered by the columns, and the columns must be unique.

LIMIT

The `LIMIT` operator is used to limit the size of a result set.

Aggregate

The Planner/Optimizer produces an `AGGREGATE` operator whenever the query includes an aggregate function. The following functions are aggregate functions: `AVG()`, `COUNT()`, `MAX()`, `MIN()`, `STDDEV()`, `SUM()`, and `VARIANCE()`.

Append

The `Append` operator is used to implement a `UNION`. An `Append` operator will have two or more input sets.

Result

The `Result` operator is used to execute a query that does not retrieve data from a table, for example, executing functions.

Nested Loop

The `Nested Loop` operator is used to perform a join between two tables. A `Nested Loop` operator requires two input sets (given that a `Nested Loop` joins two tables, this makes perfect sense).

Merge Join

The `Merge Join` operator also joins two tables. Like the `Nested Loop` operator, `Merge Join` requires two input sets: an outer table and an inner table. Each input set must be ordered by the join columns.

Hash and Hash Join

The `Hash` and `Hash Join` operators work together. The `Hash Join` operator requires two input sets, again called the outer and inner tables.

Group

The `Group` operator is used to satisfy a `GROUP BY` clause. A single input set is required by the `Group` operator, and it must be ordered by the grouping column(s).

Subquery Scan and Subplan

A `Subquery Scan` operator is used to satisfy a `UNION` clause; `Subplan` is used for subselects. These operators scan through their input sets, adding each row to the result set.

Tid Scan

The `Tid Scan` (tuple ID scan) operator is rarely used. A tuple is roughly equivalent to a row. Every tuple has an identifier that is unique within a table; this is called the tuple ID.

Materialize

The `Materialize` operator is used for some subselect operations. The Planner/Optimizer may decide that it is less expensive to materialize a subselect once than to repeat the work for each top-level row.

Setop

There are four `Setop` operators: `Setop Intersect`, `Setop Intersect All`, `Setop Except`, and `Setop Except All`. These operators are produced only when the Planner/Optimizer encounters an `INTERSECT`, `INTERSECT ALL`, `EXCEPT`, or `EXCEPT ALL` clause, respectively.

Summary

This chapter started with tuning queries and continued with how caching benefits the execution of a query. So simply writing a query and expecting a good performance is not always enough. There are multiple ways to tune queries for better performance, which we covered them in this chapter, to help you write queries. We also covered how to tweak the configuration settings to get the best performance from disks, and how to use Optimizer hints to let it choose the best plan. We discussed generating and reading Explain Plan, and each node in the Explain Plan. In the next chapter, we will cover in-built extensions in PostgreSQL, how to build contrib modules, and dblinks. These days many applications need images to be stored in their database as part of their operations, so we will also cover large objects in the next chapter.

9
PostgreSQL Extensions and Large Object Support

In the previous chapter, we talked about the process of query execution and found out what went wrong by looking at plans, then fixing it. Sometimes, a query itself could be the reason for performance issues, so we talked about tuning as well; and sometimes, it is just that some settings need to be changed to make a query perform better. We also covered available caches and how to install them as extensions. In this chapter, we will cover extensions.

- What is an extension?
- How do we create/build/install them?
- How do we use database links?
- Importing/exporting images into databases

Creating an extension

Extensions are one of the nice features in PostgreSQL. These were introduced in PostgreSQL 9.1. An extension is simply a bunch of SQL together in a script file. So, creating an extension loads the objects into the database. For example, a new datatype will require new functions, new operators, and probably new index operator classes. It is helpful to collect all these objects in a single package to simplify database management. PostgreSQL calls such a package an extension.

The following is the syntax to create an extension:

```
CREATE EXTENSION [ IF NOT EXISTS ] extension_name
[ WITH ] [ SCHEMA schema_name ]
         [ VERSION version ]
         [ FROM old_version ]
```

Let's take an example of creating a simple extension, pg_stat_statements, and the objects loaded by creating it:

```
postgres=# CREATE EXTENSION pg_stat_statements ;
CREATE EXTENSION
```

The functions created are as follows:

```
postgres=# \df pg_stat_statement*
List of functions
-[ RECORD 1 ]--------+------
 Schema              | public
 Name                | pg_stat_statements
 Result data type    | SETOF record
 Argument data types | showtext boolean, OUT userid oid, OUT dbid
 oid, OUT queryid bigint, OUT query text, OUT calls bigint, OUT
 total_time double precision, OUT min_time double precision, OUT
 max_time double precision, OUT mean_time double precision, OUT
 stddev_time double precision, OUT rows bigint, OUT shared_blks_hit
 bigint, OUT shared_blks_read bigint, OUT shared_blks_dirtied
 bigint, OUT shared_blks_written bigint, OUT local_blks_hit bigint,
 OUT local_blks_read bigint, OUT local_blks_dirtied bigint, OUT
 local_blks_written bigint, OUT temp_blks_read bigint, OUT
 temp_blks_written bigint, OUT blk_read_time double precision, OUT
 blk_write_time double precision
 Type                | normal
-[ RECORD 2 ]-----------+
    Schema              | public
    Name                | pg_stat_statements_reset
    Result data type    | void
    Argument data types |
    Type                | normal
View created:
postgres=# \dv pg_stat_statement*
List of relations
-[ RECORD 1 ]--------------
 Schema | public
 Name   | pg_stat_statements
 Type   | view
 Owner  | postgres
```

We can see that an extension is created in a `public` schema. So, if we do not provide any schema as an owner while creating an extension, it creates an extension in the schema, which is in `search_path`. If we want the extension in a particular schema, then the syntax is as follows:

```
postgres=# DROP EXTENSION IF EXISTS pg_stat_statements;
DROP EXTENSION
postgres=# CREATE EXTENSION pg_stat_statements WITH SCHEMA ext_owner;
CREATE EXTENSION
```

If you want to change the schema of an extension, you can alter the schema once it is created. You can use the following syntax:

```
postgres=# ALTER EXTENSION pg_stat_statements SET SCHEMA public;
ALTER EXTENSION
```

Compiling extensions

We talked about creating extensions in the preceding topic; however, we can only create extensions that are already compiled against our installation. We can see available extensions in the `pg_available_extensions` catalog.

```
postgres=# SELECT * FROM pg_available_extensions limit 1;
-[ RECORD 1 ]-----+-----------------------------------------
name              | adminpack
default_version   | 1.0
installed_version | 1.0
comment           | administrative functions for PostgreSQL
```

We cannot create an extension that is not already compiled, for example:

```
postgres=# SELECT * FROM pg_available_extensions WHERE  name='postgis';
name | default_version | installed_version | comment
-----+-----------------+-------------------+---------
(0 rows)
postgres=# create extension postgis;
ERROR:  could not open extension control file
"/Library/PostgreSQL/9.4/share/postgresql/extension/postgis.contro l": No
such file or directory
postgres=#
```

If you observe, `postgis` is not available in the list, so we could not create extension. So, how do we deal with such kinds of extension? For this, we will compile the source with PostgreSQL installation. Let's compile and create a `postgis` extension.

Here are the higher-level steps to install PostGIS on a Linux machine:

- Download the PostGIS source from `http://postgis.net/source/`
- Untar the file and configure it using your current `pg_config` path:

```
./configure --with-pgconfig=/path/to/your/pg_config
```

- Execute `make` and `make install` to create libraries and install binaries

However, you can find detailed installation for various platforms on `http://trac.osgeo.org/postgis/wiki/UsersWikiInstall`.

Now, let's check if you have PostGIS in the available extensions list:

```
postgres=# SELECT * FROM pg_available_extensions WHERE name='postgis';
-[ RECORD 1 ]-----+-----------------------------------------
name              |postgis
default_version   | 2.2.2
installed_version |
comment           | PostGIS geometry, geography, and raster spatial
                    types and functions

(1 row)
```

Now, if you try to create a PostGIS extension:

```
postgres=# CREATE EXTENSION postgis;
CREATE EXTENSION
postgres=#
```

In this way, we can build extensions from the source code, even though they are not in the extensions list available with the default installation.

Database links in PostgreSQL

Let's see a use case to explain why we will need database links at all. Let's say you want output from a table, function, or any other object of a database that is different to the one you are connected to. Then, generally, you will connect to the other database and fetch the data. However, if you are doing this through a function, then it will not be possible for you to connect to other databases within the function. However, using db links, you do not need to connect to that database; instead, you just access those databases using db links.

Unlike some of the other popular RDBMS databases, PostgreSQL does not have a CREATE DATABASE command. However, there are a few functions to access objects of different databases. You will need to create a dblink extension to get those functions. The syntax is as follows:

```
postgres=# CREATE SCHEMA for_dblink;
CREATE SCHEMA
postgres=# CREATE EXTENSION dblink WITH SCHEMA for_dblink;
CREATE EXTENSION
```

You will see the dblink functions using the following command:

```
postgres=# \df for_dblink.dblink*
List of functions
Schema | Name | Result data type | Argument data types | Type
-------+------+------------------+---------------------+------
for_dblink | dblink | SETOF record | text                  | normal
for_dblink | dblink | SETOF record | text, boolean         | normal
for_dblink | dblink | SETOF record | text, text            | normal
for_dblink | dblink | SETOF record | text, text, boolean   | normal
.
.
.
```

Here is an example of how to use the preceding links.

Let's establish a connection to the database before you use them:

```
postgres=# SELECT dblink_connect('test_conn','dbname=postgres');
dblink_connect
------------------
OK
(1 row)
```

In the preceding example, `test_conn` is the connection name that you can use later in the same session, and `dbname` is the name of the db you want to connect with in order to execute the queries.

To execute a query, we will use the following syntax:

```
postgres=# SELECT * FROM dblink('test_conn','select  ''testing_db_conn''')
as test(string varchar);
string
------------------
testing_db_conn
(1 row)
```

We will use the same connection, `test_conn`, to execute a query so it connects to the `postgres` database to run the query. You must specify the return datatype of the calling query to display values.

So `SELECT` works fine. How about DDL and DMLs? Let's try these:

```
postgres=# SELECT * FROM dblink('test_conn','create table  dblink_test(id
int)') as test(result varchar);
result
-----------------
CREATE TABLE
(1 row)
postgres=# SELECT * FROM dblink('test_conn','select * from  dblink_test')
as test(result varchar);
result
---------
(0 rows)
```

The same function can be used for DDLs as well. Now, let's test DMLs:

```
postgres=# SELECT * FROM dblink('test_conn','insert into  dblink_test
values(1)') as test(result varchar);
result
--------------
INSERT 0 1
(1 row)
postgres=# SELECT * FROM dblink('test_conn','select * from  dblink_test')
```

```
as test(result varchar);
result
--------
1
(1 row)
postgres=# SELECT * FROM dblink('test_conn','update dblink_test  set id=2
where id=1') as test(string varchar);
string
----------
UPDATE 1
(1 row)
postgres=# SELECT * FROM dblink('test_conn','select * from  dblink_test')
as test(result varchar);
result
--------
2
(1 row)
postgres=# SELECT * FROM dblink('test_conn','delete from  dblink_test') as
test(string varchar);
string
----------
DELETE 1
(1 row)
postgres=# SELECT * FROM dblink('test_conn','select * from  dblink_test')
as test(result varchar);
result
--------
(0 rows)
```

As per the preceding tests, the dblink function can be used for SELECT, DDLs, and DMLs.

You can check out the usage of other dblink functions on http://www.postgresql.org/docs/9.5/static/dblink.html.

Using binary large objects

What if someone wants to store a picture, Word document, or PDF, in a database? For this, PostgreSQL has a large object facility that provides stream-style access to user data, which is stored in a special large-object structure. Streaming access is useful when you are working with data values that are too large to manipulate conveniently as a whole.

The large object implementation breaks large objects into **chunks** and stores them in rows in the database. A B-tree index guarantees fast searches for the correct chunk number when doing random-access reads and writes.

How do we implement it? As this book is intended to teach you the basics, let's look at how to create/implement large objects:

Creating a large object

You can use the `lo_creat` function to create a large object. The syntax is as follows:

```
Oid lo_creat(PGconn *conn, int mode);
```

The return value is `Oid`.

Here's an example:

```
inv_oid = lo_creat(conn, INV_READ|INV_WRITE);
```

The `Oid lo_create(PGconn *conn, Oid lobjId);` function also creates a new large object. The OID to be assigned can be specified by `lobjId`; if so, failure occurs if that OID is already in use for some large object. If `lobjId` is `InvalidOid` (zero) then `lo_create` assigns an unused OID (this is the same behavior as `lo_creat`). The return value is OID that was assigned to the new large object, or `InvalidOid` (zero) on failure.

The `lo_create` is new as of PostgreSQL 8.1; if this function is run against an older server version, it will fail and return `InvalidOid`.

Here's an example:

```
inv_oid = lo_create(conn, desired_oid);
```

Importing a large object

You can use the `lo_import` function to import the large object into the database:

```
Oid lo_import(PGconn *conn, const char *filename);
```

The `filename` attribute specifies the operating system name of the file to be imported as a large object. The return value is an OID.

Exporting a large object

To export a large object into an operating system file, use the `lo_export` as shown:

```
int lo_export(PGconn *conn, Oid lobjId, const char *filename);
```

The `lobjId` argument specifies an OID of the large object to export, and the filename argument specifies the operating system name of the file. Note that the file is written by the client interface library not the server. It returns 1 on success, -1 on failure.

Writing data to a large object

To write data to a large object, you can use the `lo_write` function, as shown:

```
int lo_write(PGconn *conn, int fd, const char *buf, size_t len);
```

This writes `len` bytes from `buf` (which must be of size `len`) to the large object descriptor `fd`. The `fd` argument should be returned by a previous `lo_open`. The number of bytes actually written is returned (in the current implementation, this will always equal `len` unless there is an error). In the event of an error, the return value is -1.

Although the `len` parameter is declared as `size_t`, this function will reject length values larger than `INT_MAX`. In practice, it's best to transfer data in chunks of a few megabytes at the most.

We have taken examples from the PostgreSQL documentation; these are simple and clear. You can check out http://www.postgresql.org/docs/current/static/lo-interfaces.html#LO-CREATE to learn how to read/seek/close large objects.

Here is an example function with which you can test: http://www.postgresql.org/docs/current/static/lo-examplesect.html.

Server-side functions

PostgreSQL also has server-side functions that you can execute in database. You can connect to the database and, using SQLs, insert and fetch large objects. Let's look at an example:

```
postgres=# CREATE TABLE image_load(name text, image oid);
CREATE TABLE
postgres=#
postgres=# INSERT INTO image_load VALUES('my_image',
```

```
lo_import('/tmp/pic.png'));
INSERT 0 1
postgres=#
```

You can specify an OID while importing:

```
postgres=# INSERT INTO image_load VALUES('my_image',
lo_import('/tmp/pic.png',123456));
INSERT 0 1
```

And export it using the following query:

```
postgres=# select lo_export(image_load.image, '/tmp/pic.png') from
image_load ;
lo_export
-----------
1
(1 row)
```

Summary

In this chapter, we covered how to create, compile, and install extensions. Every extension has its own usage, so simply creating extensions that you do not use does not hurt much; however, it unnecessarily increases the count of objects in the database. As PostgreSQL is the most popular open source database, there are plenty of contrib and external extensions that are available in the market openly. Additionally, we also covered db links, which is useful when you are working with multiple databases. There are many applications that store large objects in the database, so we took a look at those as well. In the next chapter, we will cover how to connect Postgre with PHP, and how to deal with DDLs, DMLs, and SELECT with PHP. We will describe this with practical examples that will help you test yourself locally before implementing your actual requirements.

10
Using PHP in PostgreSQL

In the previous chapter, we covered what an extension is and how it's useful. We also covered how to create an extension and compile an extension that is not available by default. Additionally, we also talked about the `dblink` extension and how it is useful in the real world. The examples that we described gave you a better understanding of how those work and how to use them. In this chapter, we will work on PHP with Postgres. We start with a simple connection to Postgres with PHP and then talk about how to use DDLs, DMLs, and fetching data. We will talk about the available functions of PHP when working with SQLs.

Postgres with PHP

In this chapter, we will discuss how to use PostgreSQL with web services such as Apache/PHP, which is one of the most famous web services available in the market. In this chapter, we will demonstrate all the concepts using

- Apache/2.4.7 (Ubuntu)
- PHP Version => 5.5.9-1ubuntu4.16
- PostgreSQL(libpq) Version => 9.3.11

As the scope of the book is limited to Postgres development essentials, we hope that you have basic apache/PHP skills, which is the reason we are directly jumping into the PHP scripting sections.

PHP-to-PostgreSQL connections

To make a connection to PostgreSQL from PHP, we have a set of built-in functions where we need to pass our connection string and a set of client options to make a connection. Here, we have the pg_connect() and pg_pconnect() functions in PHP that will get the connection from PostgreSQL.

Now, let's try a simple connection to Postgres using PHP:

```php
<?php
$dbcon = pg_connect("host=localhost port=5432 dbname=postgres
user=postgres");

if (!$dbcon) {
   echo"Unable to make connection";
   exit;
}
else {
   echo"Successfully made connection to PostgreSQL\n";
}
?>
```

To run the PHP code, we need to either embed the code in an HTML file and then call the web page or we can use the PHP command-line interface.

The result is as follows:

```
$ php /tmp/test.php
Successfully made connection to PostgreSQL
```

In the preceding code, we used the pg_connect function to make a connection to the database. If this function is able to make the connection successfully, then it returns a non-empty resource and an empty resource if it fails to connect to the database.

And we also have another function, pg_pconnect(), which makes a persistent connection to PostgreSQL. Persistent connections are useful to reuse existing connections if any new connection is needed. One real use case for persistent connection is that, using the pg_pconnect() method, we can use the same database connection during multiple page reloads. There are also some caveats about persistent connections that we need to take care of. You can refer to the pros and cons of persistent connections at http://php.net/manual/en/features.persistent-connections.php.

To demonstrate a persistent connection, let's try to get the same database connection twice, as shown next.

Let's create a PHP file with the `getDBConnection()` function, which we have called in the previous chapters:

```
$ catpgconnection.php
<?php

functiongetPDBConnection() {
  $dbcon = pg_pconnect("host=localhostdbname=postgres
  user=postgres");

  if (!$dbcon) {
    echo"Unable to make connection\n";
    exit;
  }
  else {
    echo"Successfully made persistent connection to  PostgreSQL\n";
    echo"pg connection pid is "; echo pg_get_pid($dbcon);
    echo"\n";
    return $dbcon;
    }
  }

functiongetDBConnection() {
  $dbcon = pg_connect("host=localhostdbname=postgres
  user=postgres");
  if (!$dbcon) {
    echo"Unable to make connection\n";
    exit;
  }
  else {
    echo"Successfully made connection to PostgreSQL\n";
    echo"pg connection pid is "; echo pg_get_pid($dbcon);
    echo"\n";
    return $dbcon;
  }
}
?>
```

Now, let's write the `test.php` file including the preceding PHP file, as shown in the following code:

```
$ cattest.php
<?php
include'pgconnection.php';
$con=getPDBConnection();
```

```
pg_close($con);
$con=getPDBConnection();
pg_close($con);
?>
```

If you see the preceding code, we close the database connection using pg_close once we have got the database connection.

```
$ phptest.php
Successfully made persistent connection to PostgreSQL
pg connection pid is 91258
Successfully made persistent connection to PostgreSQL
pg connection pid is 91258
```

From the previous result, we got the same Postgres connection, the pid is 91258, even though we closed the connection using pg_close. Now, let's try the same code with pg_connect() and see the impact:

```
<?php
include'pgconnection.php';

$con=getDBConnection();
pg_close($con);
$con=getDBConnection();
pg_close($con);
?>
$ phptest.php
Successfully made persistent connection to PostgreSQL
pg connection pid is 91271
Successfully made persistent connection to PostgreSQL
pg connection pid is 91272
```

The moment we changed the behavior of getting a connection from pg_pconnect() to pg_connect(), we got two different connection pids for each function call. This is due to the pg_close() function that is not effective against persistent connections. If we change the connection string to pg_pconnect(), we will get a new persistent connection.

We can create an asynchronous connection to Postgres using PGSQL_CONNECT_ASYNC as an option for the pg_connect()/pg_pconnect() functions, and use the pg_connect_poll (resource) function to check connection availability. However, these functionalities have been added from the PHP 5.6.0 version onwards.

Dealing with DDLs

In PHP, we have the pg_query() function that we use to execute all kinds of SQL statement. We can use this function to execute either DDL or DML statements. This function takes two arguments; one is the db connection resource and the other is an SQL statement. To track the SQL statement status, we have the pg_last_error() function, which takes the db connection as its argument.

Now, let's try to create a test table using the preceding getDBConnection()

```php
<?php
include'pgconnection.php';

$con=getDBConnection();
$sql =<<<EOF
CREATE TABLE test(d char(1));
EOF;

if (pg_query($con, $sql)) {
  echo"test table is created successfully\n";
}
else{
  echo"Failed in creating table\n";
  echopg_last_error($con);
  echo"\n";
}
?>
```

```
$ phptest.php
Successfully made connection to PostgreSQL
pg connection pid is 91659
test table is created successfully
```

Let's run the same PHP script and see what error we get:

```
$ phptest.php
Successfully made connection to PostgreSQL
pg connection pid is 5369
PHP Warning:  pg_query(): Query failed: ERROR:  relation "test" already
exists in /tmp/test.php on line 24
Failed in creating table
ERROR:  relation "test" already exists
```

As expected, we got an ERROR saying that the relation already exists.

In PHP, we can also use `pg_execute()` to execute any DML or DDL statements. All SQL statements that we execute will get fired on the database as a single statement as an implicit transaction. We can also run the set of SQL statements explicitly as shown in the following code:

```
$sql =<<<EOF
CREATE TABLE test(d char(1));
ALTER TABLE test ADD column d2 char(1);
EOF;
```

Otherwise, we can also initiate one `pg_query()` to begin the transaction, and one `pg_query()` to close the transaction as shown in the following code

```
pg_query($con, "BEGIN");

$sql =<<<EOF
CREATE TABLE test(column1 char(1));
ALTER TABLE test ADD column column2 char(1);
EOF;
if (pg_query($con, $sql)) {
  echo"test table is created successfully\n";
  pg_query($con, "END");
}
else {
  echo"Failed in creating table\n";
  echopg_last_error($con);
  echo"\n";
}
```

DML operations

To execute a DML operation against the database, we can use a set of `pg_*` functions. We can use the same functions for all DML operations.

`pg_query/pg_query_params/pg_insert/pg_update/pg_delete`

First, let's try to insert records into the database with `pg_query`:

```
$sql=<<<EOF
INSERT INTO test VALUES('A', 'B');
INSERT INTO test VALUES('I', 'U');
EOF;

if (pg_query($con, $sql)) {
  echopg_affected_rows($con); echo " Records are inserted
```

```
          successfully";
    }
    else {
       echo"Failed inserting records";
       echopg_last_error($con);
       echo"\n";
    }
```

Result:

```
$ php /tmp/test.php
Successfully made connection to PostgreSQL
pg connection pid is 92153
2 Records are inserted successfully
```

If we want to know how many records our code inserted, then we will have to use
pg_affected_rows($con) after executing the INSERT statements.

pg_query_params

Using the pg_query_params function, we can pass a set of arguments to the SQL query.
This is the benefit of using this function over pg_query, where we can pass arguments to
the actual SQL. Additionally, the pg_query_params function accepts only one DML SQL
query, unlike the pg_query function. Another benefit we get from pg_query_params() is
that it gives protection against SQL injections. Refer to http://php.net/manual/en/functi
on.pg-query-params.php, for more details on preventing SQL injections.

```
    if(pg_query_params($con, 'INSERT INTO dummy VALUES($1, $2)',  array("I",
    "U"))) {
       echopg_affected_rows($con);
       echo" Records are inserted successfully";
    }
    else {
       // Exception section here
       ....
    }
```

In the preceding code snippet, we have used $1 and $2 to represent the field values as
arguments and array("I", "U") to represent the argument values. Here, $1="I" and
$2="U". In pg_query_params(), $1, $2, and ..$n always map to *array (value-1, value-2, …*
value-n).

pg_insert

The `pg_insert` function gives a more programmatical approach to inserting records into a table. This function takes three arguments. First one is the database connection name, second one is table name, and the last one is column name associated with table. An associate array should be `"fieldname"=>"value"`.

For example, let's use the same example we used for `pg_query_params` with `pg_insert`, as shown in the following code:

```
if (pg_insert($con, 'test', array("column1"=>"A",  "column2"=>"B"))) {
  echopg_affected_rows($con); echo " Records are inserted
  successfully";
}
else {
  echo"Failed inserting records";
  echopg_last_error($con);
}
```

Using the `pg_query()`, `pg_query_params()`, or `pg_insert()` functions, we can execute DML operations. All the approaches we see, submit the query to the database engine, and the database will parse it and generate a plan. Each time you call these functions, the db engine needs to perform these parsing and generating plans. If you execute the preceding functions in any of the loops it will become a performance issue.

To avoid this, we will use `pg_execute()` along with the `pg_prepare()` function. The `pg_prepare()` function takes three arguments, namely, connection resource, statement name, and parameterized SQL query. Here, the prepared statement name can be anything. It does not have to be related to any object name in the database. The syntax is as follows:

```
pg_prepare($con, "loopStmt", "INSERT INTO test VALUES($1, $2)")
```

Once the `pg_prepare()` execution is successful, we will get `"loopStmt"` as the prepared statement name, which we will use in all the `pg_execute()` function calls.

Here is a sample implementation:

```
if (pg_prepare($con, 'loopStmt', 'INSERT INTO test VALUES($1,  $2)')) {
  echo"Prepared statement is created\n";

  if (pg_execute($con, 'loopStmt', array("i", "u"))) {
    echo"Executed prepared statement successfully\n";
  }
}
```

Result:

```
$ php /tmp/test.php
Successfully made connection to PostgreSQL
pg connection pid is 93104
Prepared statement is created
Executed prepared statement successfully
```

Data retrieval

To retrieve records from the database, we can use the same functions that we used to INSERT records into a database, except pg_insert(). To retrieve the records or to navigate tuples one by one, we need to use some other functions where we can traverse the complete query result set.

Now let's discuss query retrieval functions one by one.

pg_fetch_all

Once we execute our SQL query using pg_execute, pg_query, or pg_query_params, we can use pg_fetch_all; this takes the data resource as an argument and returns an array, which holds our complete query result set.

The following is an example:

```php
<?php
...
$con=getDBConnection();

$res=pg_query($con, "SELECT * FROM test");
$arr=pg_fetch_all($res);

echo"Complete result set\n";
print_r($arr);
?>
```

In the preceding PHP code, we used $res as an argument for pg_fetch_all(). which is a pointer to the query result set.

Result:

```
$ php /tmp/test.php
Successfully made connection to PostgreSQL
```

```
pg connection pid is 93342
Complete result set
Array
(
[0] => Array
(
[column1] => A
[column2] => B
)

[1] => Array
(
[column1] => I
[column2] => U
)
)
```

pg_fetch_assoc

The pg_fetch_assoc function is similar to pg_fetch_all, but pg_fetch_assoc gives a much more convenient way to play with the result set. That is, using pg_fetch_all(), we will not have control over the order of columns as they appear in the SELECT statement in the result set. If we made any SQL query changes, pg_fetch_all() gives a different array with brand-new column indexes. The pg_fetch_assoc() function also takes the result set as an input and returns an associate array where the column names are keys that will give us more flexiblility while traversing the result set.

```php
<?php
include'pgconnection.php';

$con=getDBConnection();

$res = pg_query($con, "SELECT * FROM test");
if (!$res) {
  echo"An error occurred.\n";
  exit;
}
while ($row = pg_fetch_assoc($res)) {
  echo $row['column1']; echo "\t";
  echo $row['column2']; echo "\n";
}
?>
```

```
$ php /tmp/test.php
Successfully made connection to PostgreSQL
```

```
pg connection pid is 93518
a  b
i  u
```

From the preceding example, $row is an assoc array, and we used a column name as a key to get the actual record values.

pg_fetch_result

Using the pg_fetch_result function, we can fetch the required specific data value from the result set. This function takes three arguments: the result set, row number, and the required field number, as shown in the following example:

```php
<?php
include'pgconnection.php';

$con=getDBConnection();

$res = pg_query($con, "SELECT * FROM test");
if (!$res) {
  echo"An error occurred.\n";
  exit;
}

$val=pg_fetch_result($res, 0, 0);
echo"Row(0,0) $val\n";
$val=pg_fetch_result($res, 0, 1);
echo"Row(0,1) $val\n";
?>
```

Result:

```
$ php /tmp/test.php
Successfully made connection to PostgreSQL
pg connection pid is 7221
Row(0,0) a
Row(0,1) b
```

Helper functions to deal with data fetching

There are other helper functions that help you retrieve the results. Let's go through these functions one by one:

pg_free_results

Using the `pg_free_results` function, we can clear the memory resources that are used to hold the result set. All the data retrieval functions we used earlier occupy a certain amount of memory to hold the result set. It is a good practice to clear the result set after we are done processing the query results.

pg_num_rows

Using the `pg_num_rows` function, we can get the number of tuples in the result set. That is, if we execute a query, it returns the number of tuples the SELECT query has fetched from the database.

pg_num_fields

Using the `pg_num_fields` function, we can get the number of columns or fields in the result set. That is, it returns the number of columns we mentioned in the SELECT query.

pg_field_name

Using `pg_field_name` function, we can get the field name that we mentioned in the SELECT query. This function takes the result source as the first argument and the column position in the mentioned SELECT query as a second argument, which will return the column name associated with that numeric field.

pg_meta_data

Using the `pg_meta_data` function, we can get the meta information about the table. That is, we can get the complete table definition in an array format.

pg_convert

Using the `pg_convert` function, we can convert the associate array to proper SQL converted values by comparing the actual table definition.

The following is an example:

```php
<?php
include'pgconnection.php';

$con=getDBConnection();

$res = pg_query($con, "SELECT * FROM test");
if (!$res) {
  echo"An error occurred.\n";
  exit;
}

echo"Table defintion\n";
$meta = pg_meta_data($con, 'test');
var_dump($meta);

$val = pg_num_rows($res);
echo"Number of records: $val\n";

$val = pg_num_fields($res);
echo"Number of fields: $val\n";

$col1 = pg_field_name($res, 0);
echo"Column 1 is: $col1\n";

$col2 = pg_field_name($res, 1);
echo"Column 2 is: $col2\n";

$vals = array(
  'column1' =>'u',
  'column2' =>'i'
);

$stmt_helper = pg_convert($con, 'dummy', $vals);
echo"pg_convert array is:\n";
print_r($stmt_helper);
?>
```

Result:

```
Successfully made connection to PostgreSQL
pg connection pid is 7350
Table defintion
array(2) {
  ["column1"]=>
array(6) {
    ["num"]=>
int(1)
    ["type"]=>
string(6) "bpchar"
    ["len"]=>
int(-1)
    ["not null"]=>
bool(false)
    ["has default"]=>
bool(false)
    ["array dims"]=>
int(0)
  }
  ["column2"]=>
array(6) {
    ["num"]=>
int(2)
    ["type"]=>
string(6) "bpchar"
    ["len"]=>
int(-1)
    ["not null"]=>
bool(false)
    ["has default"]=>
bool(false)
    ["array dims"]=>
int(0)
  }
}
Number of records: 4
Number of fields: 2
Column 1 is: column1
Column 2 is: column2
pg_convert array is:
Array
(
["column1"] => E'U'
["column2"] => E'I'
)
```

UPDATE

As we discussed at the beginning of this chapter, to perform DML operations on a table, we can use the `pg_query`, `pg_query_params`, or `pg_update` PHP functions, by providing the respective function arguments.

The following is an example:

```php
<?php
...

$con=getDBConnection();

echo"Updating records using pg_query_params\n";
pg_query_params($con, 'UPDATE test SET column1=$1, column2=$2', array('I', 'U'));

echo"Updating records using pg_update\n";
pg_update($con, 'test', array('column1'=>'U', 'column2'=>'I'),
array('column1'=>'I', 'column2'=>'U'));
?>
```

Result:

```
$ php /tmp/test.php
Successfully made connection to PostgreSQL
pg connection pid is 7544
Updating records using pg_query_params
Updating records using pg_update
```

In the preceding example, for the `pg_update` function, we gave four arguments. One is the connection and the other is the table name. In the remaining parameters, one is the actual data and the other is the condition array. So here, actual statement executed by `pg_update` is `UPDATE test SET column1='U', column2='I' WHERE column1='I' and column2='U';`.

We can also use `pg_prepare()` to prepare update statements that we used earlier to `INSERT` records.

DELETE

To perform deletions against databases, we can use pg_query() or pg_query_params().
Also, we have alternative approaches such as the pg_delete() and pg_prepare()
functions.

The following is an example:

```php
<?php
include'pgconnection.php';

$con=getDBConnection();

$con=getDBConnection();

echo"Deleting records using pg_query_params\n";
pg_query_params($con, 'UPDATE test SET column1=$1, column2=$2', array('I',
'U'));

echo"Deleting records using pg_delete\n";
pg_delete($con, 'test', array('column1'=>'U', 'column2'=>'I'));
?>
```

Result:

```
$ php /tmp/test.php
Successfully made connection to PostgreSQL
pg connection pid is 15978
Deleting records using pg_query_params
Deleting records using pg_delete
```

In the preceding example, we used the pg_delete function, which takes three arguments.
One is the connection resource, followed by the table name and the associate array. We can
frame the pg_delete function as DELETE from test WHERE column1='U' and
column2='I'.

COPY

In PHP, the pg_copy_from() and pg_copy_to() functions are greatly helpful when
dealing with bulk data sets. With the pg_copy_from function, we can load a large data
array into a table using a single function. Similarly, we can also copy a complete table into a
single array using the pg_copy_to function. These functions actually behave like the COPY
feature that we have in PostgreSQL.

The following is an example:

```php
<?php
include'pgconnection.php';

$con=getDBConnection();

echo"Loading actual dummy table into an array\n";
$rows = pg_copy_to($con, 'test');
printf("Number of rows loaded into array is %ld\n", count($rows));

echo"Now loading the records to backup table\n";
pg_copy_from($con, 'test_backup', $rows);

$res = pg_query($con, "SELECT COUNT(*) FROM test_backup");
printf("Count of test table %ld\n", pg_fetch_resulL($res, 0, 0));
?>
```

Result:

```
$ php /tmp/test.php
Successfully made connection to PostgreSQL
pg connection pid is 32108
Loading actual test table into an array
Number of rows loaded into array is 1048576
Now loading the records to backup table
Count of test table 1048576
```

In the preceding example, we dump all the records of `test` table into the `$rows` array, and again load the complete array into the `dump_backup` table using two simple function calls.

In PHP, we can also COPY from `stdin` using the `pg_put_line` and `pg_end_copy` functions.

Let's see an example of how to read data from `stdin` for the COPY statement:

```php
<?php
...
$con=getDBConnection();
pg_query($con, "COPY test FROM STDIN");
pg_put_line("U\tI\n");
pg_put_line("U\tI\n");
pg_put_line("\\.\n");
pg_end_copy();

$rows=pg_copy_to($con, 'test');
print_r($rows);
?>
```

Result:

```
$ php /tmp/test.php
Successfully made connection to PostgreSQL
pg connection pid is 37913
Array
(
[0] => UI
[1] => UI
)
```

From the preceding results, we see the actual output of `print_r($rows)`; it prints the records using `\t` as the delimiter, which is the default PostgreSQL COPY statement delimiter. This is the reason `pg_copy_from` works with the array that was returned by the `pg_copy_to` function.

Summary

In this chapter, we used PHP with Postgres. We started with simple connections; however, we talked about the available PHP functions for DDL, DML and SELECT. For your convenience, we described each section with examples and provided PHP code that you can test yourself. We hope that will give you a better understanding of PHP. We also hope that, after reading this chapter, you will be able to prepare PHP code and execute it on your own. In the next chapter, we will talk about Java with PostgreSQL. Java is one of the most popular programming languages in the market. So many applications are designed on Java and connect to the database. We will use real-time examples to describe how and where it is useful. Additionally, we will also cover how to create a table from PL/Java and access/modify it through the code.

11

Using Java in PostgreSQL

In the previous chapter, we talked about how to make a connection to PostgreSQL using PHP; the available PHP functions to modify the database objects using DMLs and DDLs; and functions to fetch the data using SELECTs. To understand this better, we even provided examples. This gives you a basic idea about how to proceed with PHP if you want to build code based on it. In this chapter, we will make database connections using Java, which is one of the most popular programming languages in the technology world. Additionally, we will also cover how to create objects using Java, and how to manipulate data once the objects are created. We will provide some examples with sample codes, which will help you start with it. We will also talk about **Java Database Connectivity** (**JDBC**) drivers that are needed to run the Java code against databases.

Making database connections to PostgreSQL using Java

As this book is intended to give you the basics, we will start with simple Java code that retrieves data from the database. For the Java code, we should have Java installed on the machine, and we need a PosgreSQL java driver to connect it to the database.

Here is the sample code:

```
import java.sql.Connection;
import java.sql.DriverManager;
import java.sql.Statement;
import java.sql.ResultSet;
import java.sql.SQLException;


public class JavaSelect {
```

```
public static void main(String[] args) throws
ClassNotFoundException, SQLException{
   Class.forName("org.postgresql.Driver");
   Connection con =
   DriverManager.getConnection
   ("jdbc:postgresql://ip:port/dbname","user","password");
   Statement stmt = con.createStatement();
   //Queries
   ResultSet rs   = stmt.executeQuery("select * from table");
   while (rs.next()) {
      System.out.println(rs.getString("column_name"));
   }
 }
}
```

In the preceding code, we imported the sql classes available in the PostgreSQL Java driver. You can download the driver from `https://jdbc.postgresql.org/download.html`.

Let's go through the Java code:

```
Class.forName("org.postgresql.Driver");
```

This line represents the class name from the postgresql driver. It loads the main class from the driver. The class name is `org.postgresql.Driver`.

```
Connection con =
DriverManager.getConnection("jdbc:postgresql://ip:port/dbname","user","pass
word");
```

This is the connection string of the database with which you want to connect your code and execute the queries.

```
Statement stmt = con.createStatement();
```

This line declares a statement that connects to your connection string.

```
ResultSet rs   = stmt.executeQuery("select * from table");
```

Here, we executed the query using `executeQuery` and stored the result through `ResultSet`.

```
while (rs.next()) {
   System.out.println(rs.getString("column_name"));
}
```

Here, we printed the output from the results stored.

Now, let's look at a real example. We have a table, `java_test`, in the `postgres` database, and we inserted a couple of rows:

```
postgres=# select * from java_test ;
id
----
 1
 2
(2 rows)
```

Now, we will retrieve this table from Java code. Here is the code:

```java
import java.sql.Connection;
import java.sql.DriverManager;
import java.sql.Statement;
import java.sql.ResultSet;
import java.sql.SQLException;


public class JavaSelect {
  public static void main(String[] args) throws
  ClassNotFoundException, SQLException{
    Class.forName("org.postgresql.Driver");
    Connection con = DriverManager.getConnection
    ("jdbc:postgresql:
    //127.0.0.1:5432/postgres","postgres","postgres");
    Statement stmt = con.createStatement();
    //Queries
    ResultSet rs   = stmt.executeQuery("select * from java_test");

    while (rs.next()) {
      System.out.println(rs.getString("id"));
    }
  }
}
```

We have to compile the code before executing it. As we are using Linux, `javac` is the Java compiler:

```
root@ubuntu:/home/postgres# javac JavaStmtPG.java
```

It creates a `.class` file that you can execute through Java. However, as we said, it needs a PostgreSQL Java driver to execute it. We downloaded the `postgresql-9.4.1208.jre6.jar` driver for this demo. Here is how you can execute it:

```
root@ubuntu:/home/postgres# java -cp :postgresql-9.4.1208.jre6.jar
JavaStmtPG
1
2
root@ubuntu:/home/postgres#
```

So, it executed the query in the database and printed the rows.

Using Java to create a PostgreSQL table

As of now, we have explored a simple example to retrieve rows of a table with a single column. Now, lets's see how to create a table using Java.

We will use the same kind of code (with some modifications) to create the table. Here is the sample code:

```
import java.sql.Connection;
import java.sql.DriverManager;
import java.sql.Statement;
import java.sql.ResultSet;
import java.sql.SQLException;
public class JavaCreate {
  public static void main(String[] args) throws
  ClassNotFoundException, SQLException{
    Class.forName("org.postgresql.Driver");
    Connection con = DriverManager.getConnection
    ("jdbc:postgresql:
    //127.0.0.1:5432/postgres","postgres","postgres");
    Statement stmt = con.createStatement();
    stmt = con.createStatement();
    String sql = "CREATE TABLE demo_create " +
                "(ID INT PRIMARY KEY NOT NULL," +
                " FIRST_NAME VARCHAR NOT NULL, " +
                " LAST_NAME VARCHAR)";
    stmt.executeUpdate(sql);
    stmt.close();
    con.close();
    System.out.println("Table created successfully");
  }
}
```

The preceding code creates the `demo_create` table with three columns (id, first name, and last name).

If you run the preceding code, it displays the following result:

```
root@ubuntu:# java -cp :postgresql-9.4.1208.jre6.jar JavaCreate
Table created successfully
root@ubuntu:#
```

Using Java to insert records into a PostgreSQL table

We created a table using the preceding code. Now, let's insert some records into it. Again, it's the same code, but with a few modifications:

```java
import java.sql.Connection;
import java.sql.DriverManager;
import java.sql.Statement;
import java.sql.ResultSet;
import java.sql.SQLException;
public class JavaInsert {
  public static void main(String[] args) throws
  ClassNotFoundException, SQLException{
    Class.forName("org.postgresql.Driver");
    Connection con = DriverManager.getConnection
    ("jdbc:postgresql:
    //127.0.0.1:5432/postgres","postgres","postgres");
    Statement stmt = con.createStatement();
    stmt = con.createStatement();
    String sql = "INSERT INTO demo_create
    (ID,FIRST_NAME,LAST_NAME)"
    + "VALUES (1, 'Tom', 'Lane' );";
    stmt.executeUpdate(sql);

    sql = "INSERT INTO demo_create (ID,FIRST_NAME,LAST_NAME) "
         + "VALUES (2, 'Robert', 'Haas' );";
    stmt.executeUpdate(sql);

    sql = "INSERT INTO demo_create (ID,FIRST_NAME,LAST_NAME) "
         + "VALUES (3, 'Kevin', 'Grittner' );";
    stmt.executeUpdate(sql);
    stmt.close();
    con.close();
    System.out.println("Records inserted successfully");
  }
```

```
    }
```

If you run the preceding code, it inserts three records in the demo_create table:

```
root@ubuntu:# java -cp :postgresql-9.4.1208.jre6.jar JavaInsert
Records inserted successfully
root@ubuntu:# /opt/PostgreSQL/9.4/bin/psql -p 5432 -U postgres -d postgres
-Aqt -c "select * from demo_create"
Password for user postgres:
1|Tom|Lane
2|Robert|Haas
3|Kevin|Grittner
```

Using Java to update records into a PostgreSQL table

Again, to update/delete the rows from a table, you can use the same piece of code with a few modifications.

You can change the SQL statement in the preceding code to the following one for UPDATE:

```
String sql = "UPDATE demo_create SET ID=4 where ID=1;";
stmt.executeUpdate(sql);
```

Here is the sample code for your convenience:

```
import java.sql.Connection;
import java.sql.DriverManager;
import java.sql.Statement;
import java.sql.ResultSet;
import java.sql.SQLException;


public class JavaUpdate {
  public static void main(String[] args) throws
  ClassNotFoundException, SQLException{
    Class.forName("org.postgresql.Driver");
    Connection con = DriverManager.getConnection
    ("jdbc:postgresql:
    //127.0.0.1:5432/postgres","postgres","postgres");
    Statement stmt = con.createStatement();
    stmt = con.createStatement();
    String sql = "UPDATE demo_create SET ID=4 where ID=1;";
    stmt.executeUpdate(sql);
    stmt.close();
    con.close();
```

```
        System.out.println("Records updated successfully");
    }
}
```

This is the result when you compile and run it:

```
root@ubuntu:# javac JavaUpdate.java
root@ubuntu:# java -cp :postgresql-9.4.1208.jre6.jar JavaUpdate
Records updated successfully
root@ubuntu:# psql -p 5432 -d postgres -U postgres -c "select * from
demo_create"
 id | first_name | last_name
----+------------+-----------
  2 | Robert     | Haas
  3 | Kevin      | Grittner
  4 | Tom        | Lane
(3 rows)
```

Using Java to delete records into a PostgreSQL table

So far, we have created, inserted, and updated the table. Now, let's delete the rows from the table. Again, we will use the same piece of code as an example:

```
import java.sql.Connection;
import java.sql.DriverManager;
import java.sql.Statement;
import java.sql.ResultSet;
import java.sql.SQLException;

public class JavaUpdate {
  public static void main(String[] args) throws
  ClassNotFoundException, SQLException{
    Class.forName("org.postgresql.Driver");
    Connection con = DriverManager.getConnection
    ("jdbc:postgresql:
    //127.0.0.1:5432/postgres","postgres","postgres");
    Statement stmt = con.createStatement();
    stmt = con.createStatement();
    String sql = "DELETE FROM demo_create WHERE ID=2;";
    stmt.executeUpdate(sql);
    stmt.close();
    con.close();
    System.out.println("Records Deleted successfully");
  }
```

}

Here is the output when you run the preceding piece of code:

```
root@ubuntu:# psql -p 5432 -d postgres -U postgres -c "select * from
demo_create"
 id | first_name | last_name
----+------------+-----------
  2 | Robert     | Haas
  3 | Kevin      | Grittner
  4 | Tom        | Lane
(3 rows)

root@ubuntu:# javac JavaDelete.java
root@ubuntu:# java -cp :postgresql-9.4.1208.jre6.jar JavaDelete
Records Deleted successfully
root@ubuntu:#
root@ubuntu:# psql -p 5432 -d postgres -U postgres -c "select * from
demo_create"
 id | first_name | last_name
----+------------+-----------
  2 | Robert     | Haas
  3 | Kevin      | Grittner
(2 rows)
```

Catching exceptions

So far, we have examined at simple code that just executes statements, such as create, insert, delete, and update; however, we did not try to catch the exceptions.However, it is most important that you catch code exceptions in the real world. Here is simple code to capture an exception using the try/catch block:

```java
import java.sql.Connection;
import java.sql.DriverManager;
import java.sql.Statement;
import java.sql.ResultSet;
import java.sql.SQLException;

public class JavaConnection {
  public static void main(String args[]) {
    Connection conn = null;
    try {
      Class.forName("org.postgresql.Driver");
      conn = DriverManager
      .getConnection("jdbc:postgresql:
```

```
        //127.0.0.1:5432/postgres","postgres", "postgres");
    } catch (Exception exp_err) {
        exp_err.printStackTrace();
        System.err.println(exp_err.getClass().getName()+":
        "+exp_err.getMessage());
        System.exit(0);
    }
    System.out.println("Opened database successfully");
    }
}
```

The preceding example, captures connection errors if it is unable to connect to db.

For a successful connection:

```
root@ubuntu:# javac JavaConnection.java
root@ubuntu:# java -cp :postgresql-9.4.1208.jre6.jar JavaConnection
Opened database successfully
root@ubuntu:#
```

For a failed connection:

```
root@ubuntu:# javac JavaConnection.java
root@ubuntu:# java -cp :postgresql-9.4.1208.jre6.jar JavaConnection
org.postgresql.util.PSQLException: FATAL: database "postgrues" does not
exist
    at
org.postgresql.core.v3.ConnectionFactoryImpl.readStartupMessages(Connection
FactoryImpl.java:712)
    at
org.postgresql.core.v3.ConnectionFactoryImpl.openConnectionImpl(ConnectionF
actoryImpl.java:213)
    at
org.postgresql.core.ConnectionFactory.openConnection(ConnectionFactory.java
:66)
    at org.postgresql.jdbc.PgConnection.<init>(PgConnection.java:215)
    at org.postgresql.Driver.makeConnection(Driver.java:406)
    at org.postgresql.Driver.connect(Driver.java:274)
    at java.sql.DriverManager.getConnection(DriverManager.java:571)
    at java.sql.DriverManager.getConnection(DriverManager.java:215)
    at JavaConnection.main(JavaConnection.java:12)
org.postgresql.util.PSQLException: FATAL: database "postgrues" does not
exist
root@ubuntu:#
```

Using prepared statements

PostgreSQL allows the server side to prepare statements. Its purpose is to reuse the parsing and planning of statements and reduce some overhead. Here is the sample code to use `PreparedStatements` in Java:

```java
import java.sql.Connection;
import java.sql.DriverManager;
import java.sql.Statement;
import java.sql.ResultSet;
import java.sql.SQLException;
import java.sql.PreparedStatement;

public class JavaPrepare {
  public static void main(String[] args) throws
  ClassNotFoundException, SQLException{
    Class.forName("org.postgresql.Driver");
    Connection con = DriverManager.getConnection
    ("jdbc:postgresql:
    //127.0.0.1:5432/postgres","postgres","postgres");
    PreparedStatement stmt = con.prepareStatement("select * from
    demo_create");
    ResultSet rs   = stmt.executeQuery();

    while (rs.next()) {
      System.out.println(rs.getString("id"));
    }
  }
}
```

This is the output when you run the code:

```
root@ubuntu:# javac JavaPrepare.java
root@ubuntu:# java -cp :postgresql-9.4.1208.jre6.jar JavaPrepare
2
3
root@ubuntu:#
```

Loading data using COPY

To improve data loading, PostgreSQL has a COPY command that loads/unloads the data from/to a file. You can load the data using COPY from JDBC using the `CopyManager` constructor. Here is an example:

```java
import java.io.FileReader;
```

```
import java.io.IOException;
import java.sql.PreparedStatement;
import java.sql.Connection;
import java.sql.DriverManager;
import java.sql.ResultSet;
import java.sql.SQLException;
import java.util.logging.Level;
import java.util.logging.Logger;
import org.postgresql.copy.CopyManager;
import org.postgresql.core.BaseConnection;

public class JavaCopy {
  public static void main(String[] args) {
  try {
    Class.forName("org.postgresql.Driver");
    Connection con = DriverManager.getConnection
    ("jdbc:postgresql:
    //127.0.0.1:5432/postgres","postgres","postgres");
    CopyManager cm = new CopyManager((BaseConnection) con);

    FileReader fr = new FileReader("test.txt");
    cm.copyIn("COPY demo_create FROM STDIN WITH DELIMITER '|'",
    fr);
  } catch (Exception exp_err) {
      exp_err.printStackTrace();
      System.err.println(exp_err.getClass().getName()+":
      "+exp_err.getMessage());
      System.exit(0);
    }
    System.out.println("Copied data successfully");
  }
}
```

This is the output when you run the code:

```
root@ubuntu:~# psql -p 5432 -d postgres -U postgres -c "delete from
demo_create"
DELETE 3
root@ubuntu:~# psql -p 5432 -d postgres -U postgres -c "select * from
demo_create"
 id | first_name | last_name
----+------------+-----------
(0 rows)

root@ubuntu:~# cat test.txt
1 | Robert | Haas
2 | Tom    | Lane
3 | Kevin  | Grittner
```

```
root@ubuntu:~#
root@ubuntu:~#
root@ubuntu:~# javac -cp postgresql-9.4.1208.jre6.jar JavaCopy.java
root@ubuntu:~# java -cp :postgresql-9.4.1208.jre6.jar JavaCopy
Copied data successfully
root@ubuntu:~#
root@ubuntu:~#
root@ubuntu:~# psql -p 5432 -d postgres -U postgres -c "select * from
demo_create"
 id | first_name | last_name
----+------------+-----------
  1 |   Robert   |   Haas
  2 |   Tom      |   Lane
  3 |   Kevin    |   Grittner
(3 rows)
```

Connection properties

Let's talk about the connection properties. While connecting to the database using the connection string, as in the earlier examples, you can also set other parameters in addition to standard connection parameters. These properties may be specified in either the connection URL or the additional properties object parameter to `DriverManager.getConnection`. The following examples illustrate the use of both methods to establish an SSL connection:

```
String url = "jdbc:postgresql://localhost/postgres";
Properties props = new Properties();
props.setProperty("user","fred");
props.setProperty("password","secret");
props.setProperty("ssl","true");
Connection conn = DriverManager.getConnection(url, props);
```

or

```
String url =
"jdbc:postgresql://localhost/test?user=fred&password=secret&ssl=true";
Connection conn = DriverManager.getConnection(url);
```

You can go through the driver documentation (https://jdbc.postgresql.org/documentation/93/connect.html#connection-parameters) for details of more available connection parameters.

Summary

In this chapter, we talked about making a connection to databases using Java and, once that connection is established, we talked about creating objects and inserting/updating/deleting data from the objects with simple examples, which helps you understand easily and write the required Java code. We covered not only simple executions but also catching exceptions when code fails to run, which gives you a hint to further troubleshooting. We also talked about prepared statements, which reduce the overhead of parsing/planning on the server, and loading the data using COPY, which is a faster way to load data in PostgreSQL.

Index

A

anomalies, DBMS
  common patterns 65
  delete anomaly 62
  first normal form (1NF) 63
  insert anomaly 62
  second normal form (2NF) 63
  third normal form (3NF) 64
  update anomaly 62
ANSI isolation levels
  explicit transaction, using 77
  implicit transaction, using 77
  isolation level, changing 76
  transaction isolation levels 76
array constructors
  about 29
  ARRAY_AGG() 32
  array_dims() 32
  Array_length() 34
  ARRAY_UPPER() 34
  string_t0-array() 31
array
  about 28
  constructors 28
  JSON 37
  slicing 34
  splicing 34
  UNNESTing, to rows 35
  XML, using in PostgreSQL 41
Atomicity, Consistency, Isolation, and Durability
    (ACID)
  atomicity 70
  consistency 71
  durability 71
  isolation 71

B

binary large objects
  creating 158
  data, writing to 159
  exporting 159
  importing 158
  server-side functions 159
  using 157
Block Range Index (BRIN)
  about 92
  reference link 92

C

cache, cleaning
  pg_buffercache extensions, using 130, 131
  pg_prewarm extensions, using 132
cached data
  optimizer setting 133, 135
chunks 157
common patterns
  hierarchy 66
  many-to-many relationships 65
  recursive relationships 67
composite datatype
  about 42
  altering, in PostgreSQL 44
  creating, in PostgreSQL 42
  dropping, in PostgreSQL 45
connection properties 190
constraint exclusion
  about 109, 116, 117, 118
  foreign inheritance 120, 122
  horizontal partitioning 118
  PL/Proxy 119
constraints
  about 83

check constraint 97
check constraints 96
exclusion constraints 98
foreign key constraint 93
NOT NULL constraints 97
unique constraints 94, 95
COPY command
used, for loading data 188
count function
reference link 13
cursors
about 10
closing 12
creating 10, 11
using 11

D

Data Manipulation Language (DML) 8, 83
datatypes
conversion between 27
DBMS
anomalies 61
DDLs
dealing with 165
design rules
data efficiency imposing ability 60
data integrity imposing ability 60
future changes accommodation ability 61
problem solving ability 59
relationship support ability 60
required data holding ability 60
DML operation
executing 166
pg_insert function 168
pg_query_params function 167
driver documentation
reference link 190

E

exclusion constraints 98
execution plan 144
explain plan
complex example 145
generating 144
reading 144

running 144
simple example 145
explicit locking
about 78
rows, locking 78
tables, locking 80
extension
compiling 153, 154
creating 151, 152, 153

F

first normal form (1NF) 63
full text search
reference link 88

G

Generalized Inverted Index (GIN) 88
Generalized Search Tree (GiST) 88
GROUP BY clause
using 12

H

HAVING clause
arguments 14
parameters 14
using 14
helper functions
COPY function 176
DELETE function 176
pg_convert function 173
pg_field_name function 172
pg_free_results function 172
pg_meta_data function 172
pg_num_fields function 172
pg_num_rows functions 172
UPDATE function 175
used, for dealing with data fetching 172

I

index
about 83
B-Tree indexes 86
clustering 92, 93
full text indexes 88

GIN 91
GiST indexes 91
hash indexes 91
multicolumn indexes 90
partial indexes 88
primary key indexes 84, 85
standard indexes 87
unique indexes 85, 86
isolation levels, transaction
dirty reads 73
phantom reads 75
unrepeatable reads 74

J

Java Database Connectivity (JDBC) 179
Java
exceptions, catching 186
used, for creating PostgreSQL table 182
used, for deleting records into PostgreSQL table 185
used, for inserting records into PostgreSQL table 183
used, for making database connections to PostgreSQL 179, 181
used, for updating records into PostgreSQL table 184
JSON, querying
containment 38
equality operations 38
key/element existence 39
output, obtaining 40
JSON
about 37
data, inserting in PostgreSQL 37
querying 38

L

LIMIT clause
using 15

M

Manage External Data (MED) 120
materialized views
about 8
benefits 8

read-only 8, 9
updatable 8, 9, 10
writeable 8, 10
max function
reference link 13
min function
reference link 13

N

normalization 61

O

optimizer setting
for cached data 133, 135
Outer join
about 22
full outer join 25
Left outer join 23
right outer join 24
types 22

P

partitioning
about 103
alternate methods 113, 114, 115
list partition 109
types 109
partitions
adding 111
implementing, on table 104, 105, 106, 107, 108
managing 111
old partition, purging 112
persistent connections
reference link 162
pg_partman extension
reference link 113
pg_query_params functions
reference link 167
PHP-to-PostgreSQL connections
creating 162
PL/Proxy
reference link 119
PosgreSQL
databases connections, making with Java 179
PostGIS Install Guide

reference link 154
PostgreSQL 9.5.3 Documentation
  reference link 130
PostgreSQL Java driver
  reference link 180
PostgreSQL table
  creating, with Java 182, 183
  records, deleting with Java 185
  records, inserting with Java 183
  records, updating with Java 184
PostgreSQL
  about 5
  composite types, altering 44
  composite types, creating 42
  database links 154, 156, 157
  databases connections, making with Java 181
  documentation, reference link 159
  JSON data, inserting 37
  triggers, adding 48
  triggers, modifying 53
  using, with PHP 161
  XML data, inserting 41
  XML, using 41
prepared statements
  data, loading with COPY 188
  using 188
psql 11

Q

query operators
  about 146
  Aggregate operator 147
  Append operator 147
  Group operator 148
  Hash Join operator 148
  Hash operator 148
  Index Scan operator 146
  Limit operator 147
  Materialize operator 149
  Merge Join operator 148
  Nested Loop operator 148
  Result operator 147
  SeqScan operator 146
  Setop operator 149
  Sort operator 147

Subquery Scan operator 148
Tid Scan operator 148
Unique operator 147
query tuning
  about 125
  cache, cleaning 129, 130
  cache, tuning 127
  hot, versus cold cache 126
query
  implementing, multiple ways 135

R

records, retrieving
  about 169
  pg_fetch_all, using 169
  pg_fetch_assoc function, using 170
  pg_fetch_result function, using 171

S

scalar subquery 17
second normal form (2NF) 63
self join
  about 21
  using 22
stale statistics
  optimizer hints 139, 143
  Optimizer hints 141
  used, for bad query performance 137, 139
subqueries
  arguments 19
  correlated subqueries 18
  existence subqueries 19
  parameters 19
  used, for returning multiple rows 18
  using 16
sum function
  reference link 13, 14

T

table partitioning 99, 100, 103
third normal form (3NF) 64
transaction isolation
  about 73
  levels, implementing 73
transactions

and savepoints 72
ANSI isolation levels 75
Atomicity, Consistency, Isolation, and Durability (ACID) 70
concurrency, effects 71
deadlocks, avoiding 77
defining 69
explicit locking 78
isolation 73
trigger function
  creating 55
  testing 56
triggers
  about 47
  adding, to PostgreSQL 48
  existing triggers, viewing 57
  modifying, in PostgreSQL 53
  removing 54

U

Union join
  using 20, 21
UPDATE operation clauses
  using 15

V

views
  about 5
  creating 5
  creating, commands 6
  deleting 7
  replacing 7

X

XML
  data, inserting in PostgreSQL 41
  data, querying 42
  using, in PostgreSQL 41